To Susc

Tendest Regards

Simon

THE SELF-TAPPING SCREW

THE SELF-TAPPING SCREW

The Recollections of a Borstal Officer

Simon Barlow

Book Guild Publishing

Sussex, England

First published in Great Britain in 2013 by
The Book Guild Ltd
Pavilion View
19 New Road
Brighton, BN1 1UF

Typesetting in Garamond by
YHT Ltd, London

Printed and bound in Great Britain by
CPI Group (UK) Ltd, Croydon, CR0 4YY

A catalogue record for this book is available from
The British Library.

ISBN 978 1 84624 844 3

Dedicated to my late son, Martin

Contents

Prelude

I had been the manager of shoe shops for eleven years. To say I hated it would be an understatement. I was paid a pittance and was seldom able to take a day off. I had a lovely wife and two small sons, but was unable to spend much time with them. I had no car and was commuting to London each day at huge cost. I complained to my area manager that I could no longer sustain the cost of rail travel and he invited me to a meeting with him and his manager to talk this through. At the meeting, the area manager told me that he had a solution; I was to be appointed manager of the Ashford branch. I pointed out to him that I didn't have a car and there was no direct rail access from Rochester to Ashford.

'It's the same county! Take it or leave it!' he replied.

Like a twit, I took it.

The journey was horrible. It consisted of a train ride to Strood, change to the Medway Valley line, then a half a mile walk to the main line station to catch a train to Ashford. None of the connections ran on time and the journey took hours. One evening, having locked the shop up at 5.30 p.m., I ran for the train as usual and just managed to catch it. Within a few minutes, however, it went into the sidings. I had to walk back along the rail lines only to find that the next train was not due for over an hour. I then resorted to the local pub with some of the local retail managers. We had a great time, but I couldn't contact home as we didn't have a phone (there were no mobiles in 1975). I caught the first train available and arrived home about two hours late, to find that my wife had had a particularly nasty miscarriage. Fortunately, the neighbours had helped her, but I wasn't there. I knew things had to change.

Thankfully, in those days, shops didn't open on Sundays, otherwise I would have never seen my family, but there was little else to smile about. Even on Boxing Day I had to attend the shop to prepare for the winter sale. It was a rut from which I saw no escape. I had no trade skills and apart for long forgotten A-levels, could not boast any formal qualifications. I knew that I had to support my family, but I had had enough. I had to get out.

I started scouring the papers and eventually applied to become a milkman. I was thrilled to be accepted and pictured myself on my round, just a stone's throw from my family. It all came to nothing when I found out that my 1966 driving licence didn't cover me for electric vehicles.

I then saw an article in the *Daily Mail* stating that prison officers were paid more than doctors (taking their overtime into consideration) and were provided with free housing. I contacted the Home Office and requested an application pack, which duly arrived.

I filled in the application form and various other documents, which – among other information – asked if my grandfather was a Communist. After putting it in the post I began to think that just maybe I had been handed a ladder to help me climb out of my desperate rut.

Within a few days I received an acknowledgement of my application, stating that they were going to write to my employers for a reference and inviting me to sit an exam, attend a medical and undergo an interview in Maidstone the following week.

I duly turned up at Maidstone prison at the appointed time, knocked on the 12-foot wooden gate and an officer opened it. I showed him my Home Office letter and he grunted then led me to a waiting area that looked as if it hadn't been decorated since the prison was built in 1812. I watched people and vehicles coming in and out of the gate lodge and the officer never varied his grunt, yet nobody seemed to have difficulty understanding him. I became transfixed, thinking that I had come across a completely new form of communication.

After about an hour, an officer with one pip on his shoulder took me to the visits room. I was sat down and a test paper was put in front of me. I was then told that I had thirty-five minutes to answer all of the questions. If I passed, I would go to the hospital wing for a medical. The test was taxing, largely due to the time constraints, but I passed nonetheless.

Then to the medical! I was expecting an attractive nurse, but was confronted by a prison officer who looked as if he could have successfully tackled Jonah Lomu. He pointed out the 'H' on his lapel, which apparently indicated that he was a hospital officer and qualified to carry out a medical. I wasn't too reassured.

He told me that at 6 foot 4 inches I was exactly what the prison service was looking for and proceeded to check all my bits, surprisingly successfully. He then sat me down in front of an eye test board. My heart sank; you would need good eyes to see through my glasses, as I am extremely short-sighted. He asked me to remove my glasses and read from a script on the wall. I removed them and couldn't even see the wall, let alone the script. When I told him that I couldn't quite read it he told me to put my glasses back on, read it, read it again and when I had memorised it I should take my glasses off and tell him what it says. I passed!

After this success only the interview remained. I was escorted to the boardroom where I was greeted by three people behind a huge oak desk. At this point I was knackered. The first question was why I wanted to join the prison service, which was followed by, 'If you say that you want to help people, I'll have one of the dog handlers set their dog on you.' A daunting start but I held my own. At the end of the interview I was told that I would be recommended and would hear from the Home Office in the next few weeks.

About a month later, the area manager visited my shop and told me that the company had received a reference application. He was furious that I was obviously not showing loyalty to the company and wanted to transfer me to a smaller shop. I subsequently found myself in a tiny shoe shop in a small town in Kent with a turnover of 20% less than I was used to. The months went by in this sleepy shop and I heard nothing from the prison service. Eventually, after two years of pressure from my employers, I phoned the Home Office and told them that I was no longer interested. Three days later, I received instructions to report to Rochester Borstal in four weeks. This was to be followed by training at Leyhill Officers Training School in Gloucestershire four weeks later. I practically skipped to the shop to hand in my notice, but this was not to be the last that I heard from my vengeful employers.

In the seventies, shop managers were subject to a bonding scheme where stock was covered by insurance in case the manager ran off with the till. However, when I left, my last month's salary and my holiday pay were withheld to cover stocktaking shortages over the years. I was subjected to the company security department investigating me and threatened with court action, simply because I had the nerve to leave.

What Have I Done?

In September 1980 I presented myself at Rochester Borstal. I was met at the gate and as I was escorted through, I saw borstal boys being marched to their duties and shouted at by uniformed officers.

God, what had I let myself in for?

On my first day, I was told that I would be assisting in escorting a borstal boy to court. At the time all prison service establishments were responsible for transporting any detained persons to court and for staffing the court docks. My first encounter with this was to escort a borstal boy to Tottenham Magistrates Court in a taxi. I was in civvies and had no idea of what I was supposed to do. To make matters worse, while trying to turn into Lordship Lane, a motorist decided that our taxi had cut him up and slewed his car in front of us. The officer in charge drew his stave, got out of the taxi and put a huge dent in the car's bonnet. I sat, cuffed to the prisoner, wondering what I would do if he decided to take it further. Fortunately, following a tirade from the officer who told him that he would be charged with aiding a prisoner to escape, he drove off.

The following day, we were introduced to the borstal system and how it worked. The boys (known as trainees) were sentenced to borstal training. This consisted of being locked up in the borstal for between six months and two years. The actual release date was determined by their personal officer and based on their behaviour. They were given a target date of nine months, but they could earn time back and be released at six months if they behaved well. However, if they refused to toe the line they could be held for two years. It was a bizarre system.

The boys were always released on a Wednesday. But so often Mum would turn up at the borstal gate at 9.00 a.m. on the due release date only to find that her little treasure had upset his officer on the previous day and had his target date removed. That meant that he would be released sometime in the next year or so, depending on the behaviour of the trainee.

While serving time, the trainees were offered courses in motor mechanics, plumbing, bricklaying, carpentry, welding, concrete moulding, farm stock management and general farm work. They also had to attend education two nights a week to achieve their qualifications.

Each morning, they would march from the wings to the parade ground, leaving only those boys who had been signed off sick and one officer on the wing. They would then line up in wing order in front of the orderly officer, the chief officer and the governor, while the orderly officer took a roll call. It was a bit like a stalag if the roll was not correct; they could stand there for hours while all the buildings were checked. When the orderly was happy, he would order the boys to form parties. Each party officer would take a position on the parade ground and his party would form lines in front of him. I say *him* because in those days only men worked in male establishments and women in female ones.

On the order of the chief, the boys would break from the ranks within their wings and shuffle to stand to attention in front of their party officer. Once the orderly officer was satisfied that all the boys were where they should be, he would order the party officers to march their parties to work. This routine was highly disciplined; if they went out of step they were likely to be put on a minor report. This was heard by the wing principal officer who could deprive them of up to three nights' association or impose a fine.

Once acquainted with how the system worked, I spent a day in the workshops. The most impressive of these was the engineering shop. The array of machinery and lathes would shame the most up-to-date private engineering firm. The opportunities were endless, but when I asked the instructor if the precision bolts and other fixings that I watched the lads produce were used in the institution, he looked embarrassed. The workshop could produce most items that the works department required, but the Home Office procurement policy dictated that all fixtures had to come from approved suppliers. Consequently, the boys' efforts were photographed and then put in the scrap metal bin. Some things don't change!

I spent another four weeks at the borstal before going to the OTS (Officers Training School). I had started with a guy called Dave who was young and well meaning, but a little bit green. Being without a car, I travelled with Dave to Leyhill each Monday and home for the weekend. I quickly discovered his secret skill: he could sleep while he was driving. He didn't just nod off; his head slumped to his chest and he snored and drifted from lane to lane. I knew when he was dozing off, because our speed would begin to exceed 90 mph. However, dangerous driving aside, he developed into a good prison officer and became a great friend.

Training

We arrived at Leyhill, a magnificent Elizabethan manor house, for the first time in September 1980 and were shown into a large reception room with the Andy Williams Christmas Show playing on the television. We were told to stay in the room and leave our bags in the corridor. Some minutes later, we were summoned to the parade square to be told that a package had been found and it was ticking. The bomb squad was called and they found an alarm clock in a holdall. Dave, completely unaware of the panic that he had caused, later admitted that he had innocently packed his clockwork alarm clock.

After the drama had died down, we were invited to choose our uniforms from the back of a lorry that had appeared in the car park. As we dug into the supply, it became clear that the Home Office only dealt with midgets. At 6 foot 4 inches, the trousers hung at least 4 inches above my shoes, leading to my borstal nickname of 'Socks'.

Our section was the first to have a female PO (Principal Officer Trainer), Miss Brown. She was brilliant, but slightly unsure of herself. In those days, men worked in men's prisons and women worked in female prisons, so it was not always easy for her and the trainees didn't always do what they could to help. However, I thank this lady from the bottom of my heart for her unselfish transfer of knowledge. Our first exercise was for two of us (designated as officers) to lead the rest of the section (twenty 'prisoners') around the manor house and not lose anyone (bearing in mind that this building contained priest holes). We marched them round the building and they, having been briefed well, created various distractions to sabotage the exercise. Within minutes, the twenty were reduced to four. As we marched our remaining four prisoners, we passed a classroom with twenty NEPOs in (New Entry Prison Officers) who had not yet been introduced to their tutor. We convinced them that, as their first exercise, they should walk with us to familiarise themselves with the building. We then delivered twenty back to our check point. Mission accomplished!

There were about 120 NEPOs on our course, broken up into six sections. Each section was undergoing training separately, but about once a week all sections were summoned to the lecture theatre. On each occasion, there would be some six students missing. It slowly occurred to us that if a student was not considered up to scratch he/she would not be summoned. It was when everyone else was in the lecture theatre that they would be escorted off the premises, armed with a one-way travel warrant, never to be seen or heard from again.

The training was intense, with many of the exercises aimed at getting us to understand the mind-set of the criminal. I remember, early in the training, being shown a Canadian film that claimed that a criminal could be identified by their high-ridge brows. Having high-ridge brows myself, I found this to be a bit of a generalisation.

As if the knowledge of the criminal justice system that we were expected to absorb wasn't taxing enough, there was also the dreaded phys. con., as it appeared in the programme, otherwise known as physical control. The initial training in phys. con. consisted of twisting various limbs belonging to your fellow students until they complied with your instructions. I found this great fun as I am double-jointed and could break out of most holds. The two PEIs (Physical Education Instructors) who were hosting these sessions put up with me for a week, but on the second Monday they invited me to demonstrate my dexterity, with them acting as the officers. The exercise left me a lot less pleased with myself and resulted in a visit to the college nurse's room. No one mentioned that they were both second dan in jujitsu, but it is a lesson that I will never forget.

We were also taught to march during the training. Why? I don't know, but this was not my forte. Every morning, we congregated on the parade ground and were taught to march in three ranks around the grounds. My brain could not handle the concept of the arm going forward and the leg going backwards. They referred to it as tic-tacking, with the right arm going in the same direction as the right leg.

Each day, one of us was chosen to be in charge. When it was my turn, it all went well, with my section in uniform marching in perfect formation, but then my mind began to wander. The instructor screamed at me when the front rank was heading for the moat. I managed to right wheel, but we were within inches of the front rank falling to an uncertain future.

Another aspect of the course was MUFTI (Minimum Use of Force Tactical Intervention) training. We were given a helmet with visor, a 3-foot stave and a shield with two hooks on the back to allow you to hang it from your left arm. Unfortunately, when you came across an immoveable object, the back of the hook would hit you in the ribs and render you in pain for the next couple of days. I have never seen so many bruised and broken ribs.

On the first day of MUFTI the weather was below freezing, so I wore a thick polo-neck jumper that my mother had knitted for me years before. After a couple of hours of charging up and down, I felt as if I was cooking, with sweat running down my back and steam visibly rising into the air. My main problem was that my glasses kept steaming up. I was charging something behind my shield, but I couldn't see what it was.

We were then sent into the gym, where the instructors would sling rolled-up plimsolls at us. We charged them, fending them off with our inadequate shields – not the preparation we needed for the riots of the eighties and nineties.

In addition to the formal training, every student had to undertake the duties of student orderly officer. This involved being in charge of the training school and sorting out any problems, or contacting the chief officer in the case of an emergency. When I was given my duty day I realised that it clashed with our section night out, so I asked around and found someone to cover for me. I then went to the chief officer to inform him that I had swapped duties. He told me in no uncertain terms that part of my training was to follow my detail and that I would fulfil my duty on that night. However, all the senior staff went home by 7.00 p.m., so it seemed that it would be fairly safe to ignore the order.

On the night in question, I kept my uniform on until 7.00 p.m., when the guy I had arranged to swap with turned up. He informed me that he was going to bed, but would leave the bleeper on. So, off we went to the local pub and got wrecked. I can't remember the details for obvious reasons, but I'm sure that it was a good night. On our return, however, we found a Hillman Imp in our parking space. We surrounded the car and saw a bloke hiding behind the seat. Being fuelled by the local beverage, it seemed a good idea to put the car on the roof. So we did. Not wanting to tackle four drunken Rottweilers, the guy soon gave himself up and we took him to the orderly room in the college for questioning. He admitted that his accomplice was dropping bottles of alcohol to the open prison next door and I called the police, who attended and arrested our Imp driver and his friend.

Before I could speak to the police I had to try to sober up and went back outside to the snow-covered grounds. Running around the building was a 5-foot deep, dry moat. Walking drunkenly past a tree at the top of the moat, an owl flew at me, screaming and I went head-first down the precipice, briefly knocking myself out. On waking, probably only a few seconds later, I managed to clamber up the side of the moat, feeling surprisingly sober, and returned to the orderly room, covered in mud and snow, before being questioned by the boys in blue. I didn't do too badly and ended up conducting a decent interview.

The following morning, we were told to attend the lecture theatre and I was convinced that I was facing the sack, having ignored the chief's orders. Everyone was looking to see who was missing and I was intrigued to see what happened to the NEPOs who disappeared, as I was convinced that this would be my fate. Oddly, for the first time, there were no faces missing. Everyone seemed confused as to the purpose of this gathering.

When the chief officer arrived at the rostrum and fixed his eyes on me all I could think about was what I was going to tell my wife and what I was going to do when I got sacked. After what seemed like an age, he said that he had an important announcement to make regarding the previous night. I thought that that was it. I had burned my bridges with my previous employers. With two young children and a mortgage, I had no chance.

He cleared his throat and stated that the prison service and the Home Office were proud of the student orderly officer who had dealt with the incident the previous night and that I would receive a commendation from Willie Whitelaw for devotion to duty. I never did receive this, but was pleased to know that I was still employed.

That evening, we were called to the snooker room to learn to supervise prisoner association. Two of the NEPOs had been allocated as officers and everyone else was a prisoner. The instructor had secretly handed one of the 'prisoner' trainees a handgun, which had to be handed around without being detected. I arrived late because I had had my first aid certificate exam, and had no idea of the point of the exercise. I have always had a fascination with guns and when someone put the pistol in my hand I examined it and then showed it to all my peers. The instructor looked at me as if I were simple and gave up the exercise.

As we neared the only long weekend in the two-month course the snow was getting deeper and we were told that if we chose to go home and could not get back we would be thrown off the course and have to re-apply. Nobody was going to keep me from my family and, fortunately, Dave agreed. So, we left on Thursday afternoon. The snow had started to thaw and we had an uneventful journey, other than Dave's annoying snores as we hurtled down the M4, at 90 mph.

I spent a very pleasurable weekend with my family, with my two sons wondering who the strange bloke was, and on Sunday, having consumed one of my wife's Sunday roasts, I waited for Dave to pick me up. The weather forecasts had been awful, stating that huge amounts of snow would be falling in the south, but as we left it was cold but dry. We set off knowing that once we had cleared central London Dave could relax and have a good sleep on the M4. But when we got onto the M4 at Reading it started. The snow was so heavy that you couldn't see the bonnet of the car. Fortunately, most people were being sensible and driving at about 15 mph in single file. Occasionally, some idiot would hammer down the hard shoulder, leave the road and disappear into a snowdrift like cotton wool.

We arrived at Leyhill about 8.00 p.m. We slept in small dormitories with six beds. When I opened the door and put my bag on my bed, there were two bodies in it. 'Sorry mate,' the trainee whispered. 'I didn't go home because of the snow.' He never explained the appearance of the naked female who got out of the bed and ran out of the room. He is now a senior governor. Maybe I should have done things differently.

At the end of the course, we were told that there would be a cross-country run on the Friday before we were given our postings. All NEPOs would take part, with no excuses. We were taken out for a recce that afternoon and it was frightening. The grounds had a large lake, which was reasonably flat, but it was about three quarters of a mile around. That was okay, but as we passed the main building the slope grew into a hill and it went on, uphill for what seemed like miles. Not being the most athletic of people, having merely walked the circuit, I was near to death and all

I could think about was a pint. I had played rugby in my early twenties, but as a shop manager, I certainly had not honed my body to perfection. Indeed, any activity was normally followed by a fag.

On looking at the notice board, I saw that the assistant governor's exam clashed with the cross-country run. I had no intention of applying for this post, as they earned about half the salary of the average prison officer with overtime. But it did give me a way out of the dreaded run.

The last duty on the Friday was to receive our postings. We were told that these were non-negotiable and that we could either accept them or leave. I was posted to Rochester Borstal, where I had started, so there was not a problem, but others were not as lucky.

Taff, who became a very good friend in later years, lived in the Welsh valleys. His wife ran a sweet shop and his twin daughters were studying for their A-levels. When we filled in the preferred options form he wrote, 'Anywhere but London.' He was posted to Brixton. There was no flexibility in the postings, so he took the posting and his marriage broke up. He later met a lovely women and is still married to her.

One guy who was posted to North Sea Camp on the east coast dressed the doll used for first aid training in prison uniform and waited on the third-floor minstrels' gallery for the chief officer to walk through the main door. After about two hours, the chief arrived with the principal and our friend screamed, 'Where the fuck is North Sea Camp?' and threw the uniformed dummy off the third floor. The chief and the principal retreated to their offices and called the emergency services. They arrived in about fifteen minutes, by which time it had all been cleared up and nobody on duty knew anything about it, but they were shown to the principal's office. It is not known what was said, but he had a very late night.

Another student, who came from Tyneside, was posted to Parkhurst on the Isle of Wight. Another guy, who came from the Isle of Wight and was posted to Accrington in Northumbria, agreed to swap. This was vetoed by the chief and they were told that their postings were non-negotiable. They both left the profession – a huge loss to the prison service.

Things got easier from this point. The training was more focussed on us taking up our postings. I already had a house on which I was paying a mortgage, but I had to obtain permission from the governor to live in it. It is difficult to believe now, but then, if an officer was posted from the OTS and had nowhere to live, the prison would buy a house in the local area.

One of the last pieces of training was to prepare us for Crown Court. A virtual courtroom was set up and we were taken through various scenarios, including rub-down searching the defendants, restraining violent prisoners and how to address the judge and other court officers. It became apparent that a tier three, high court judge was a powerful figure; we were told of occasions when dock officers who did not comply with the judge's instructions were sentenced to a day in the court cells for contempt. This training would come back to bite me in the future at the Old Bailey.

The final day at the OTS was the passing out parade. The whole course, now down to about 100 students, was to be marched onto the parade ground to be inspected by the director general who was one hell of a man. He had lost an arm and an eye as a tank commander during the Second

World War and although disabled, his bearing demanded respect and everyone in the prison service had the greatest affection for him.

For the first time in eight weeks at Leyhill the day went well. Even I managed to keep my feet and arms doing what they should and completed the march successfully. This was followed by a formal dinner, the details of which are long forgotten as we were all thinking about going home.

Dave and I returned to Rochester and as usual, Dave had a peaceful sleep on the M4 despite the fact that he was driving. It was now the week before Christmas; I was broke and looking forward to all this overtime that I had been hearing about, but I also longed to spend some time with my wife and sons. We had been given a week off between the end of the course and taking up our new duties, but I rang the detail office at the borstal to see if there was any overtime on offer. I was asked to work twelve hours every day throughout the Christmas period. Upon negotiation, I got Christmas Day off. I was told by my new colleagues that despite having a wage of £70 per week, we could take home £300 by working twelve hours a day for twelve days, starting duty at 6.15 a.m. and finishing at 9.15 p.m.

Borstal

The borstal system was founded by Sir Evelyn Ruggles-Brise. The first borstal was named after the village of Borstal, situated about two miles from Rochester and built by the boys in 1908. It is a shame that this system doesn't exist now, as it offered vocational training, education and a huge lesson in self-discipline. I am friends with many tradesmen who were saved by the borstal system teaching them a trade.

The residential units were known as houses and later as wings. There were three wings of one hundred cells, one housing trainees in dormitories, a 1960s block holding about 90 trainees, a hospital wing and a segregation unit for the most unmanageable inmates.

Well before my time, the boys would be marched from the house to the gym at 6.30 a.m. They would work out and then have a freezing cold shower. They would then return to the wing for breakfast. When I arrived in 1980 the same system was still in operation – except with the introduction of hot water.

The gate lodge displayed a framed picture of Sir Evelyn, which by the end of each day had phlegm running down the glass frame. It had become a tradition with the older borstal officers to spit on his picture as they went off duty. I hasten to add that I never took part in this practice.

Most of the officers working there had joined more than

twenty years before and knew the system inside out. They tolerated no trouble from the boys and gave all new staff a hard time.

When I joined the borstal I was attached to B Wing, which was effectively a prison within the borstal, housing long-term YPs (young prisoners). On B Wing the discipline was managed under prison rules rather than borstal, which were completely different. Working under two completely different criminal justice systems in the same day was totally confusing. When a prisoner offended against prison rules he was placed on governor's report, which would be heard by the duty governor in the segregation unit the following day. However, if a borstal boy transgressed he could be put on a minor report or a governor's report, or in serious offences he could be referred to the BOV (board of visitors). The board of visitors was a body of people who were answerable only to the home secretary. They would adjudicate on the most serious breaches of prison discipline and could over-turn a governor's decision, which they frequently did. However, I quickly learned that a borstal boy or a YP would be offered the choice of 'my punishment or the governor's'. Most would accept yours as they did not want to lose days. More on this later.

We worked for twelve days a fortnight, taking every other weekend off (if not working overtime), as did the governor and his deputy. The weekend staff members were referred to as gov. or dep., depending on which weekend you worked. I worked the dep.'s weekend.

Overtime was fiercely sought after by all officers and at the end of each shift we would examine the boards outside the orderly room to see if we had overtime the following day. These duty boards were known as the Wailing Wall.

Certain officers, known as cowboys, would work twenty-four hours a day, seven days a week if they could and would complain to the detail SO (Senior Officer) if they felt that they were not given their fair share of overtime. This was a pointless exercise as the SO in question, known as the Screaming Skull, as that is how he looked, did not believe anything anyone said to him.

On one occasion, during the heavy snow, I was on a rest day and as we were trying to sell our house, I had taken a sledge to the DIY shop about three miles away to buy paint and various other bits. While I was out my wife received a call from the Skull offering me overtime. She explained that I was out and that she would ask me to ring back when I returned. He shouted at her, 'I know he's there and if he hasn't got the bottle to come to the phone I'll have him next time I see him.' We had words the next day, but I didn't get any overtime for a week. He was the officer who was shouting at the boys when I first walked into the borstal.

My first duty on the day after Boxing Day was as visits' runner. This involved escorting borstal boys to spend half an hour with their long-suffering mothers/fathers/girl-friends, etc. My first call was to inform me that B16745 Smith in C Wing has a visit. I walked to the wing only to be told that he had gone to work on the farm. The borstal was spread out over about 70 acres and I was not familiar with its layout, but with the enthusiasm of someone new to the job, I walked out of the borstal and spent half an hour walking around the farm shouting his name.

Eventually, the farm manager asked me what I was doing. I told him and he explained that Smith had gone to the weekly gym session as he was entitled to do.

I walked back to the borstal and went to the gymnasium,

which was situated about as far from the gate as you could get. I spoke to the PEIs in the gym who said that Smith had ripped a muscle and had been sent to the hospital. I turned around and went to the hospital wing where the officer on duty looked at me and burst out laughing. I had been walking around the borstal for two hours looking for someone who didn't exist. I had probably walked several miles looking for this guy. I had been introduced to prison humour!

After this, the first two weeks of duty passed quickly. As it was the Christmas holiday season, the workshops and the education block were closed, so the time was taken up with various activities with the inmates.

B Wing

As already stated, B Wing held long-term, often violent YPs. The staff members were selected for their experience and tenacity; therefore, I was extremely flattered that I was chosen to work with these officers. However, it was confirmed years later that I was allocated there simply because of my size.

The principal officer on the wing, Bill (or sir to his friends), was completely bonkers. No one ever knew what he would do next. I would find my cap attached to the wall with a 6-inch screw pierced through it or I would put it on by the peak only to find that he had unpicked all the stitches. In those days you were not allowed to leave the wing without a cap, so I would spend the rest of the shift looking like Benny Hill's Mr Scuttle. When, later, the time came for Bill to recommend, or not, my successful completion of probation, he told me not to go to lunch as I was to play him at snooker on the wing table. If I won, he would recommend a further three months. If I let him win, I would be confirmed in the post.

He would often disappear and leave a notice on his office door, which read, 'Gone Fishing'. It was a brilliant piece of reverse psychology because he really had gone fishing right in the middle of his shift. The governor and the chief officer would do their daily rounds, look at the PO's message posting and ask, 'Where's the PO?'

Whoever was on duty would say, 'He's gone fishing.'

The governor was convinced that we were covering for him, but because of the difficult prisoners that we were dealing with, and the fact that he really didn't want to get involved, he preferred to ignore Bill's unexplained absences.

There were also two senior officers on the wing who managed the day-to-day running of the wing, supervising the staff and sorting out any unforeseen problems.

My SO was Robbie, a man's man who became a good friend. Robbie would not tolerate any disobedience from inmates and expected his staff to enforce prison rules, albeit with a strange sense of humour. The other staff members were hugely experienced and appeared to me, as a newcomer, to be afraid of nothing. One of the officers, with whom I worked the most, was known as Ram, or sometimes Psycho. He had long, blond hair, a well-trimmed beard and looked as if he should be jumping off a long ship in the eighth century with a sword in his hand.

During this holiday period, largely due to the inmates' boredom, a fight broke out. The alarm bell was pushed and the first one in was Ram who, during the melee, received a punch on the nose. He and I were manning the 'ones' – the catwalk that skirted the first landing. There were inmates shouting threats of violence, refusing to return to their cells and I was standing there trapped in this confused atmosphere of violence, thinking, 'Oh shit!' And then this Viking appeared, running along the landing with blood pouring out of his nose. He shouted to each inmate, 'Get in your fucking box or I'll put you in it!' Needless to say, they all went away without argument after that. Lesson number two learned!

Ram's normal declaration at bang up (the end of association) was, 'Happiness is door shaped; make yourselves happy.' This man was as hard as nails, but he had a soft side. For example, there was a large Afro-Caribbean inmate on the wing who couldn't read and write, but was too ashamed to go to education and ask for help. Ram would disappear for long periods and no one knew where he was. It later transpired that he was teaching this bloke to read.

On an average day at the borstal the majority of the boys were put to work and only the sick and the cleaners were returned to the wing from the parade ground. The lame and lazy were locked up and the cleaners put to work. The only staff on the wing were the senior officer, the censor officer (who sorted the mail) and the cleaning officer (whose task it was to make sure that the cleaning party scrubbed the wing from end to end). Prisoners returning from the segregation wing were also returned to the wing during the day and immediately locked in their cells.

Early on in my career at the borstal, I was allocated the job of cleaning officer for the day and another officer, Colin, was in charge of the wing. On this particular day, we were about to get the cleaning party out of their cells when the gate opened and the segregation officer shouted, 'Two on!' and shut the gate behind him. He had dumped two of the biggest and most violent West Indian prisoners I had met in my short career on the wing and it would fall to us to get them to their cells somehow. Colin and I stood behind the snooker table, as these two 6-foot, 6-inch brothers approached us. It was obvious that they had no intention of going to their cells.

Colin, who could talk his way out of being hung, said, 'Now then, you need to think what you are doing as we are so highly trained that I could put you in your cell with one finger and the other arm tied behind my back.'

I looked at him in disbelief. I had never come across two people with that much muscle and aggression and I have to confess that I was frightened. As they approached it was like a scene from *High Noon*, but due to his rhetoric, Colin defused the situation and even bet a Mars Bar on his claim. The brothers asked him to prove his boast. Colin walked around the snooker table, looking the biggest brother in the eye, then put his hand down the back of his trousers, withdrew his finger with a bit of faeces on it and shoved it under the prisoner's nose. They ran to their cells after that with no argument.

We were summoned from the officers' mess, during our meal break, to attend a cell in B wing, where a prisoner was 'smashing up' and threatening to set fire to his cell. On arriving, an experienced officer, Arthur, took charge, and with a mattress drawn from the stores, directed us to follow him and another officer. He opened the cell door and charged the prisoner, protected by the mattress. As five of us landed on him, a long thin plastic blade came through the mattress, just missing Arthur's throat. We subdued the prisoner and dragged him to the segregation unit. On investigation, it transpired that the prisoner had broken a neon light diffuser in the shower room, giving him a 30-inch-long plastic blade.

Mr Eric, (more of him later), was in charge of security. He exclaimed that he had designed a secret weapon that would prevent a reoccurrence of this incident. He proudly presented himself on the wing, a few days later, with the aforesaid weapon. It consisted of a mattress screwed on to a 6 by 4 sheet of plywood, with two wooden handles on the back. I have never seen a man in uniform look so pleased with himself.

A few days later, a prisoner, holding a piece of broken glass, was threatening to cut any officer that unlocked his door. Mr Eric turned up with his secret weapon and with two officers behind it, a third opened the cell and the makeshift assault unit charged. Unfortunately, the sheet of plywood was wider than the cell door. The two brave officers went off sick, with shoulder injuries and Mr Eric crept out of the wing, unseen. The prisoner was laughing so much, he didn't even try to resist and was removed without further trouble. The secret weapon would find useful employment later.

Shifts

There were two main shift systems across the prison system: FGS (Functional Group System) and V scheme (Variable shifts).

The training and dispersal prisons (which housed the most dangerous category-A prisoners) and the borstals operated the FGS shift scheme to cover the main part of the day in order to keep the institution running (i.e. labour movement, visits, serving meals and evening association). The early shift was from 6.30 a.m. to 1.30 p.m. The late was 12.30 p.m. to 9.15 p.m. The main was from 7.30 a.m. to 5.15 p.m. The dreaded X shift was from 7.15 a.m. to 8.15 p.m. The latter was the shift that the shirkers took as sick leave. It was known as X-shiftilitus. As we worked every other weekend, we were entitled to two rest days per week, one being a weekend day. The weekday rest day was when one would earn some serious overtime.

The V scheme was worked by the local prisons, those institutions that housed remand prisoners and ran the Crown Courts. It mainly consisted of main shifts, as the manpower was needed to run the courts and the prison during the main part of the day. Officers would work twenty weeks in the prison and twenty in the courts. There was no evening association for remand prisoners in the London prisons, so the need for evening staff was minimal. There was also what was known as the milk run.

31

When the London courts sentenced young people to six months DC, Detention Centres (the short, sharp shock of the Thatcher regime), they would be dispersed across the country. A bus would leave at the end of court and set of to deliver these wretches to DCs located from Kent to the north-east coast, the officers not getting home until the sun came up, a popular overtime earner. We always had the option of working our rest days in the London Crown Courts, because in those days the prison service deliberately ran on two-thirds of the staff that they needed, knowing that the greedy buggers, such as I, would fill the gaps, saving them the cost of uniform, NI payments, quarters and pension contributions etc.

It was assumed that you were available to work on your scheduled time off unless you put your name in the unavailable book for a particular shift. There were officers who refused to work any overtime and I always felt envious of these people, but I could not afford to join them; I had a young family and large debts carried over from my previous life.

On your rest days you could be called in for any duty, but it was almost always court duty, and after my first escort to a London Magistrates' Court I began to question the sanity of the system. The lad was accused of stealing a BMX bike. Two of us reported for duty at 7.00 a.m., collected the inmate from the wing, boarded a private taxi and were driven to Tottenham Magistrate's Court. We sat doing nothing for most of the day and his case was eventually heard at about 3.00 p.m. He pleaded guilty and was given a sentence of 'Return to Borstal'.

We got in the taxi and were driven the 30 miles back to the borstal, arriving at about 6.00 p.m. I later found out that, at the time, the only sentence that the magistrates could impose was 'Return to Borstal'. This sentence did not affect the inmate's release date; it was merely registered on his list of pre-convictions. This particular escort involved two officers, working eleven hours each at time-and-a-half, the hire of a taxi for a 60-mile round trip, nine hours waiting time and the cost of the court staff. Although the borstal system finished nearly thirty years ago, the same pointless practices still exist within adult prisons, with life-sentenced prisoners, having to be produced for offences like 'Drink Driving'.

Another little earner was the bed watch. This would occur either for booked surgery on an inmate at the local hospital or when an inmate was sick and (in the opinion of the duty hospital officer) required hospital treatment. When a lad complained of appendicitis it could normally be translated as, 'I want to abscond and it's easier to do so from the hospital than the borstal.' This quest was supported by the fact that only one officer was sent out with an inmate on a twelve-hour shift; when the officer went to the loo or for a bite to eat the inmate was unsupervised.

On my first bed watch, the lad was in an open ward next to a French window. I sat next to the bed, crossing my legs, not daring to leave him. In the next bed was a Chinaman who didn't appear to know where he was and couldn't speak English. He kept trying to get out of bed and was led back by the nurses. As luck would have it, a police officer arrived shortly after we did, escorting a drug user who had over-dosed. We agreed that we would have a half hour break each and keep an eye on each other's prisoners. I went first and had a meal in the nurses' canteen. When I arrived back on the ward it was mayhem. The police officer was standing

33

there swearing and the Chinaman was hiding under the blanket, refusing to move and screaming. The police officer had targeted the wrong bed. My prisoner had climbed out of the window and was long gone.

The Home Office was always harping on about prison officers maximising their expense claims and absences, which they labelled 'Spanish practices'. I can now see their point, but there was nothing Spanish about them, some examples of which were as follows.

If an officer was called in on a rest day to take an inmate out on escort, full expenses were paid after five hours out of the institution. Some of these escorts were to local Magistrates' Courts or hospitals. We were always transported by a local taxi (God knows what that cost) and we could be heading back to the borstal before the five-hour cut-off. The driver would pull into a lay by and we would wait until the five hours had passed and then return to the institution.

We got to know who suffered from extreme X-shiftilitus, as mentioned earlier, and if we hadn't been called in on a rest day and knew one of the sufferers was on an X shift, we'd turn up in uniform, telling the orderly officer that we'd misread the detail. The orderly officer would nearly always tell us to stay on to cover the X-shiftilitus sufferer, giving us twelve hours overtime at time-and-a-half.

One Saturday in May 1982, I received a phone call at about 6.00 a.m. It was the skull. He said, 'This is an emergency and I don't want any arguments. Get yourself up to the nick in the next hour.'

I asked how long I was required for and he replied that he couldn't answer that and I should just present myself for duty. I duly got dressed and undertook the twenty-minute walk to the borstal, having told my wife, who was expecting to spend a pleasant spring day with her husband and sons, that I probably wouldn't be long. Arriving at the borstal, we were mustered into the boardroom where the chief told us that IRA prisoners had virtually destroyed Albany Prison, on the Isle of White, the previous day and had been dispersed to various prisons around the country, most of which were not equipped to house high-status, category-A prisoners. Our brief was to report to Canterbury Prison, collect an IRA prisoner and transport him to Leicester Prison. Bearing in mind that I had never seen an adult prisoner, other than in the Crown Court, I didn't really know what to expect.

We were driven to Canterbury in the crew bus by Ram, who had the severe hump because he had been detailed to drive the bus to Leicester and bring us back, thus keeping him out of the action.

We arrived at HMP Canterbury at about 9.00 a.m. to be told that the 'Jam Sandwich' (a popular name for a cat-A van, because it had a red stripe down the length of the vehicle with a yellow stripe either side) was on its way from HMP Winchester. We were told to wait in the officers' mess and would be contacted. Poor old Ram; not only did he miss out on the action, but also on a fairly handsome breakfast.

Some two hours later, we were summoned to reception and saw three police cars parked outside, sporting enough weaponry to start a civil war. I was cuffed to the prisoner and we were locked in the van with PO Bill (sir to his friends), an SO, Dave (he of the M4 sleepover), and nothing more than wooden staves to protect us.

A police chief inspector gave our driver a radio and told him that we would not be stopping for anything. The driver replied that it was a brand new vehicle and he could not exceed 50 mph. The officer said, 'Okay,' with a wry smile on his face.

As we left the gate lodge at Canterbury and turned onto the main road, police motorcycles completely blocked the road, a helicopter appeared above our van and off we went. The convoy consisted of a lead police car, two motorcycle outriders, our van and two armed police cars bringing up the rear. There was also the police helicopter still hovering above. When the convoy met with anything that would slow us down (e.g. an old couple crossing a zebra crossing), each vehicle would sound its siren. As each vehicle had a different sounding siren, the collective noise was frightening and we must have caused many a heart attack or stroke.

As we left Canterbury, we headed for London along the A2 (the M25 had not yet been built), reaching mind-boggling speeds, with the van driver muttering that his new vehicle would never be the same, but he wasn't the only person our convoy upset that day.

Anyone who has used the Blackwell Tunnel will be familiar with the dog leg in the middle of it, apparently put there to stop the horses bolting when they caught sight of the light. As we entered the tunnel, there was a red Ford Fiesta on the left, driven by a young lady who was obviously confused by what was going on. The motorcycle outrider slowed to allow the convoy to pass and the Fiesta moved to the right to avoid it, finding herself caught between the armed police car and the van. When the blue lights started flashing and the sirens sounded, the poor girl found herself hurtling through the tunnel at about 60 mph. After a few minutes, she took her hands off the steering wheel, slammed them over her eyes, screamed and crashed into the dog leg. I often wonder if she ever got over it and, indeed, if she ever drove again.

We also gave a group of football supporters a scare as we progressed up the M1. It just happened to be FA Cup final day and we saw a Ford Anglia with a Liverpool scarf tied to its aerial and beer cans flying out of the windows. The motorcycle outrider signalled the driver to pull over, only to be met by a load of abuse. The motorcyclist dropped back to be replaced by the rear car who came up alongside the Anglia, pointing its weaponry at the driver. I have never seen anyone sober up as quickly or comply with instructions so readily.

We arrived at HMP Leicester without further incident and the prisoner was duly handed over. It is interesting to note that the prisoner and Bill (sir to his friends) slept through the whole journey.

The Farm

The farm was situated about 100 yards from the gate lodge. It had a dairy herd of about sixty cattle and a pig-breeding area. In those days, the prison service was self-sufficient in pork, milk and beef. Some years later, some idiot at the Home Office decided that it would be a good idea to privatise them so that there would be no husbandry training for prisoners and all the produce would have to be bought in. The civil servant concerned probably went on to work in the banking sector.

There were two farm-work parties: Farm 1 and Farm 2. Farm 1 was for the more trusted boys who were learning animal husbandry and, in effect, running the farm under the farm staff, unsupervised by officers. Farm 2 consisted of twelve London boys who didn't want to be there, had never seen a cow in their lives and didn't see why they had to clear up semi-frozen cow shit. The Farm 2 party was given to new officers, which included me.

We were issued with the dreaded and dangerous Phillips pocket phones for outside parties. There were two units; one for transmitting and one for receiving. These were housed in two holsters draped around the neck. To send a message you had to keep the two units away from each other to avoid feedback. So, having received a message, you took the transmitting unit from the holster around your neck then, holding the receiver at arm's length, pressed the transmit button on the other unit. However, when you pressed the transmit button, the aerial would shoot out and go straight up your right nostril. You could always tell a new officer as he would have a nasty swelling on the right side of his nose and blood stains around his mouth. When you had sent your message, you had to hold the transmitter at arm's length and hold the receiver to your ear and then alternate holding the transmit and receive unit away from your body. A lengthy exchange would appear to an onlooker as if you were demonstrating semaphore.

As party officer of Farm 2, I would march my party to the parade ground and then out of the gate to the farm. It was freezing, but being a new, naïve officer I didn't pick up the link between the temperature and the seniority of the party officer. Lesson three!

On my first day, I was told by the farm manager that the farm was to be inspected the following day by someone from the Home Office and that my work party was to spend the day pulling nettles out from the perimeter fence. The boys were not happy when I told them. I remember one saying, 'Stick an exhaust pipe in my mouth and let me taste London. I'm pissed off with all this green.'

It was a long day, with each boy complaining of stings with every single nettle they pulled out, despite the fact that they were wearing industrial gloves. I would estimate that the ten boys pulled out about four nettles during the course of the entire day.

To cheer myself up, I thought that I would have a fry-up in the mess for my tea as I was on evening duty. I ordered it by phone from the farm manager's office and immediately felt better. After marching the boys to their wings, I walked the short distance from the borstal to the mess, salivating over the fry-up I was about to consume, but when I sat down with my knife and fork I was served a mixed meat salad. I complained to Debbie, the mess cook. She said, 'This is good for you.' Good for me? A salad? I still couldn't feel my feet because of the cold.

She died some years ago, but I'm glad she wasn't my mother. You didn't mix with Debbie.

There were certain advantages of being the farm party officer; one of which was the produce. The sows would roll onto the piglets and occasionally smother them. I would then take them home and roast them. I have not tasted anything like them before or since.

Every now and then, a lorry would turn up at the farm to transport the mature pigs to the abattoir. A few days later, another lorry would arrive with the carcases. There was a refrigerated building on the farm housing the carcases of the cured pork. I never knew how to get into it, but sides of cured pork would go missing on a regular basis. There were several investigations, but to no avail. It wasn't me and I shall say no more on the subject.

As the weather got warmer, the party got more compliant, but I noticed that they would march from the borstal dressed like Eskimos and return at lunchtime in shorts and T-shirts. This was suspicious. So, one day, I told the party that I would be gone for five minutes and went to the office above the gate lodge armed with a pair of binoculars. I saw the boys strip off about three sets of shirts and jeans and drape them over the farm wall. Seconds later, a car pulled up, took the garments and drove off. I later learned that punks would pay anything for prison shirts and jeans. These were the days of Ian Dury and the shirts were on sale at Petticoat Lane Market for £40 a time. From then on I insisted that the boys showed me their shirt tails on parade.

The spring passed and I was relieved that the frozen cow shit clearing was over. I was looking forward to the late summer days, when the party would be gathering grass on the tractor and transporting it to the silage pit. As it warmed up, however, I was taken off the farm party and allocated to 8 party, where I had to patrol the industrial area. I later found out that an officer with twenty-five years of service was always allocated in the summer, but refused to take the party in the winter. He was the union rep and nobody argued with him.

One of the risks of leading an outside party is that, every now and again, one or several of the boys would decide that they would leg it up the M2 and return to London. 'Fixed posts' was announced over the radio when this was reported by the party officer and staff members were expected to proceed to their predetermined posts to look out for the absconding boy.

There were two main flaws to this plan. The first was that few officers carried a radio, so they would be blissfully unaware of the situation. The second was that some fixed posts were outside local pubs, overlooking the M2, which always proved more popular than the local train station or the river crossing. In a 'fixed post' situation, one particular ale house, with a good view of the Medway Valley, would fill up with screws in uniform. On one occasion, the lad gave himself up at about midday. The officers bought him steak and chips, plied him with ale and finally radioed the borstal that he had been recaptured at about 11.30 p.m. The following morning, he was unable to answer the charge at governor's adjudication due to his hangover.

On another occasion, the party officer had reported that he was one inmate short. A member of the public phoned in to say that she had seen a young man taking off borstal clothing and starting to swim the River Medway, heading for Snodland Village. We arrived at Snodland Station, having previously arranged for British Rail to turn off the power to the railway lines, and searched the area. As we searched, we heard faint cries of help. 'Sir! Sir, come and help me.' We followed the cries to a travellers' camp behind the station and saw him standing in an iron bath tub with five middle-aged travelling women trying to pull his trunks down to give him a wash. We saved him by a matter of minutes.

Within the grounds of the farm was Fort Borstal. It was part of Palmerstone's Napoleonic defences of Chatham and was connected by a still-visible ammunition railway to two other nearby forts: Cookham and Bridgewood. It was blocked off by two huge steel gates, the key to which I would borrow on my weekends off to take my two young sons there. It was a magical place. There were huge arches where legend had it that some officers had built a sea-going boat out of materials requisitioned from the borstal, but I could not comment further. There were tunnels leading to who knows where, a railway line running along the escarpment that looked over the River Medway from 450 feet up, pheasants, foxes, woodpeckers, bats and so many other forms of wildlife that had been undisturbed for over 150 years, save the odd bit of boat building. We used to sit there for hours on a sunny day, the boys learning more about wildlife and history than they would ever have learned in school.

8 Party

When I was moved from Farm 2 to 8 party, my duties involved reporting the number of inmates in the area, following parade and making sure that the area was clear at the end of labour. It was the most mind-numbing job that I have had in my twenty-five years. I used to spend most of my time walking around the perimeter fence, checking on the birds' nests and picking mushrooms. I would then patrol the workshops, including the laundry, concrete-moulding shop, bricklaying shop and the sports field. In that area there was also a carpentry shop; it was a large shed situated behind the bricklaying shop and I had no idea that the place existed for a long while, even though I patrolled the area every day. The chippy was named Don. He would walk past and say, 'Anything to report?' I then had to keep my eye on him, as he would pick up a brick and throw it at me. I never worked out why. Once, as he was carrying a wrecking bar, I foolishly told him that I had had an operation on my right knee some three years earlier. He tapped my knee cap with the wrecking bar and as I collapsed, trying not to be sick, he said, 'They didn't do a very good job, did they,' and then walked off whistling!

The 8-party area was separated from the borstal by a 20-foot-high gate and there was a similar gate leading from 8 party to the lane, running down the side of the borstal. Oddly enough, this gate had the same lock as the 8-party gate. Confusingly, Dave (not the M4 sleeper, but another with the same name) would regularly offer to swap duties and I would bite his hand off. I later found out that he was reporting the party numbers, following parade and then letting himself out of the external gate, going home to his quarter 200 yards away, having a couple of cups of tea and a kip and returning in time for the inmates to return to the wings.

On one occasion, in mid-winter, I had been patrolling the perimeter of the sports field (albeit looking for wildlife and mushrooms) and was freezing cold. I walked up the side of the laundry and saw the chief and governor inspecting the area. I cut through the alleyway between the laundry and the brick shop, bidding the chief and the governor a good day, and the chief said to me, 'Just as I thought; you spend your shift drinking tea in the laundry. See me at 09.00 hours in my office tomorrow.'

I could accept his mistake, but I was the only idiot who really did patrol all day. The others sat in the laundry drinking tea or went completely AWOL like Dave, (not the M4 sleeper).

The following morning, as instructed, I was standing outside the chief's office with my tunic buttoned up and cap on, with the peak over my eyes, looking, as I thought, every bit the perfect officer. I tapped reverently on the chief's door and at that point Colin walked by. He said, 'You should take the upper hand,' and kicked the door to the point that I thought it would come off the hinges. He then ran off.

The chief opened the door, looked at me with total distain and said, 'In a hurry, Mr Barlow? I think not.' He then left me standing there for three hours. At 12.00 p.m. he opened the door and asked me why I had not fulfilled my duties that morning. I tried to protest, but he just said, 'Go away.' This gave the wing staff a great subject for hilarity. Looking back, it was a good lesson in the borstal mind-set and I was determined that Colin would get his a few years later.

One day, at the end of labour, I counted out one less inmate than I had counted in. I was getting constant messages on my nostril-destroying radio to report that my numbers were correct, as nobody could go to lunch until the roll was confirmed, but I didn't reply; I didn't want to admit to losing a borstal boy so early in my career. I decided to stop and think where I could have gone wrong and as my mind replayed the entire shift, I heard a faint cry of a distressed inmate. It took me about ten minutes to track the sound down to the carpenter's shop. As I opened the door, I was faced with a large Afro-Caribbean chap with his head in the vice and his overalls secured to the long bench by 3-inch screws. Despite his situation, he seemed pleased to see me. I released his head from the vice and he shed his overalls. I asked him what had happened and he replied, 'I didn't put any sugar in Don's tea, but he'll be alright in the morning.' And off he toddled. Nobody got a lunch break that day and I can't remember my explanation.

There was a motor mechanics' shop on the site, where the boys were trained in mechanics, panel beating, paint spraying and re-upholstering. The great news for the staff was that a lottery was held to decide who would provide a car for the boys to work on. The winner could buy a sixties wreck and walk away with a new car for the price of the parts. I came third, behind the administration officer (AO) who was on the senior management team, in charge of finance and all things clerical. His job was to monitor all financial transactions to the suppliers of the borstal, including staff wages and overtime. I later found out how annoying this man was, but more of this later.

I waited about a year for my turn, but after the AO had driven away his pristine MK1 Cortina his conscience was obviously pricked; he ruled that the lottery was a conflict of interest and that the practice should cease – my first experience of the mind-set of the modern civil servant.

Absconds

Although the borstal was a secure establishment, with so many outside parties, some inmates were bound to try to abscond. As mentioned earlier, each wing had a nominated officer who carried a radio, with a call-sign of 'Foxtrot' and when an abscond was reported the radio controller would call, 'Fixed posts'. The nominated officer would immediately go to his abscond post, which would be quite interesting if he was halfway through serving lunch. This was an extremely popular duty and the nominated officer would take no persuading to man his post; most were based in country pubs, as the absconders would very often head cross country. Most of them were Londoners, so they got lost and were easily caught. For some odd reason, I always got the fixed post outside Chatham Station where there was no pub, but a large metal building that blocked all radio signals.

On one occasion, an inmate had run away from the swimming pool and I was sitting opposite Chatham Station with an officer popularly known as Slippery. We didn't expect to have to respond, but then the missing boy appeared around the corner, wearing only a pair of swimming trunks.

Slippery leapt out of the car and jumped the absconder. I tried to follow, only to find that he had left the child lock on. By the time I had wound the window down and extricated all 6 foot 4 inches of me, several minutes had passed, but I managed to join the affray. He was clearly not going to give up easily. Slippery had him in an arm-lock and I held his head with one arm, leaving me to call for help on the radio, but the bloody building was not allowing us to transmit. We were left rolling around with the lad in the middle of the main road outside the station in full uniform and could hear comments like, 'Oh look, Mable. I wonder what they're doing.'

Eventually, a man asked us if he could help. We explained that we were prison officers apprehending an escapee and asked him to call 999. This he did and at last we received assistance.

On another occasion, two SOs, Rob and Allen, were out looking for a new car. They had been around several dealers in Maidstone and decided to look in Strood. As they were driving along the M2, two borstal boys appeared, running down the bank. Rob stopped the car on the hard shoulder and told them to stay where they were.

Thinking fast, they split up, one running towards the motorway bridge and the other towards the woodland, southbound. Allen, who was not what you would describe as an athlete, chased the first and Rob the second. Allen managed to keep up with his prey until they reached the bridge (about a mile and a half away). At this point, Allen was knackered; he was on his last legs, he could hardly see, he was thinking that he was going to throw up and his legs ceased to work. He ground to a halt, holding the central barrier rail to stop him collapsing. To his surprise, the boy stopped as well. He walked up to Allen and said, 'I didn't know that you people were so fit. You may as well take me back.'

Allen couldn't answer. Still clinging onto the rail, he

thought that he was going to pass out. He couldn't talk or breathe. The lad helpfully sat on the verge and waited for some considerable time until Allen had enough energy to wave at a passing police car.

Meanwhile, Rob had taken off after the other one. Rob was fairly fit and gave the boy a run for his money. The boy ran onto the cattle bridge that spans the motorway and Rob decided that he would cut him off by leaping over the fence. What he didn't add in to the calculation was the barbed wire neatly hidden by the hedge. As he did his Superman impression, his trousers caught on the wire, reducing them to ribbons. It also caused him to stop dead, in mid-air, resulting in him crashing down to earth and landing on his nose. To most people, this would not be too much of a problem, but if anyone reading this has ever had sight of Rob's nose they will be able to picture the scene. The lad stopped running, came back to help Rob out of the barbed wire and put his nose in a sling. Both boys were charged with absconding, but the authorities went easy on them under the circumstances.

Wing Duties

As time went on, I started to spend time on the wing as cleaning officer. After parade, the only inmates who were unlocked were the cleaning party. The party comprised the hotplate crew, who would assist staff in serving meals and would be required to scrub out the dining area, clean out the heated trolleys and wash up the trays. The others would scrub the landings by hand, on their knees, with four boys at one end of the wing and four on the other, scrubbing towards each other. If it was not satisfactory, they would be required to do it all again.

The inmates were locked in their cells for twelve hours and each morning the wing would be unlocked by section (about fifteen cells at a time). The boys would then slop-out their pots and conduct their other bodily functions. They were only allowed two trips to the recess (the area with slop-out drains, toilets and fresh water). After getting rid of the waste they would collect water for shaving and teeth cleaning, etc. They were all issued with a Wilkinson Sword razor blade, which would be collected before they had their breakfast. When an inmate was at risk of self-harm he would be issued with a locked razor, from which the blade could not be extracted without a key.

Breakfast consisted of porridge (the consistency varied from soup to concrete depending on who was on duty) or cornflakes, three slices of bread and a knob of butter. On

Sunday they were served bacon and eggs, but Sunday was the only time that they were allowed to have a lie-in. As the servery was only open for half an hour, they would have to choose between a cooked breakfast or an extra hour in bed, so only about half of them would turn up, giving the staff a hearty breakfast.

Once the inmates had gone to work the officer would conduct a 'locks, bolts and bars' (LBBs) check. This involved a close inspection of the internal walls, the window bars and the door locks of each cell, which would then be signed for in the wing log. This was a laborious task, as there were over 100 cells. One officer, who I shall not name, but whose name began with T, always gave us junior staff constant lectures on how important LBBs were and told us that most escapes could be prevented by vigilant inspections of cells. He would later be found wanting, but more on this later.

Another duty of the cleaning officer was to collect the food from the kitchen, divide it into portions to match the number of inmates and control the servery.

The food was actually very good, but there were two main problems. Firstly, an inexperienced officer would often not control the portions properly and allow the inmates to take more than their share. Secondly, the amount of food collected from the kitchen was sometimes not enough to feed the amount of inmates on the wing. This was usually the case with chips, so the cleaning officer had to return to the kitchen and wait for more chips to be cooked, thereby holding up the running of the whole institution as none of the officers were allowed out of the institution for lunch until all the wings reported that all inmates were locked up. I was sure that neither of these scenarios would apply to me...

On my first sojourn as cleaning officer, the morning went well, the wing being duly scrubbed with little trouble from the inmates. I then took the hotplate crew to the kitchen feeling rather pleased with myself and collected the midday meal of sausage, egg and chips (a particular favourite of the guests). We returned it to the serving area of the wing and I stood behind the servery, supervising the portion control. At first the inmates were lined up in an orderly queue, but I sensed that something was going on as there was much whispering. Then, suddenly, a fight broke out in the queue. Being big and keen, I leapt over the hotplate instead of pushing the alarm bell to summon staff, but I felt that I could handle the situation without help. When I confronted the two who were fighting they stopped and apologised. However, when I returned to the hotplate I found that all of the sausages had been nicked and every inmate in the queue had a knowing smile on his face. I then had to return to the kitchen to face the senior officer caterer (who was known as Boss Hog, as he had similar aspirations to the character in the seventies TV series, *Dukes of Hazzard*) to ask for 200 extra sausages. His questioning was painful, but I eventually got the food an hour and a half later, which meant that all staff missed their lunch. I learned that day that prisoners can spot a new screw a mile away, in the dark – a lesson that I passed on throughout my career. However, I had obviously not absorbed the lesson on that day.

During association that evening, I was supervising the shower room. The boys would roll up with their shower kit and were given five minutes to get themselves clean. It was part of my job to make sure that they didn't overrun, so that all the inmates could have a shower. That evening, the first lad out said, 'Excuse me, sir, could you open my cell door?'

This I did, especially as he was so polite. Everyone who came out of the shower made the same request, to which I duly complied. About ten minutes before the end of association a rather cross Rob pointed out that the wing rules stated that all cell doors were to be kept locked during association and not opened until lock up. This was to avoid theft and dealing.

I duly went around the wing, closing the doors that I had recently opened and the inmates were not impressed. Many had left their towels in their cells and were dripping wet. I was not Mr Popular, but they knew that they had had me over and they also knew that I had had a bollocking from Rob and that I could not give in to them. As I would not give way and reopen their cells, I think that this was the point where I was starting to gain respect.

And then there were shit parcels! The wing was divided into eight sections. Halfway down both landings was a recess, where the inmates would slop-out and wash. The cells either side would form a section: four on the ground floor and four on the twos. If anyone threw a shit parcel out of a cell window their whole section would lose their association for that evening. A shit parcel consisted of the inmate defecating in a piece of newspaper (or anything else to hand) and throwing it out of the window. This resulted in an officer with a party of boys having to clean the excrement from outside the wing the following morning.

The loss of association worked well for a short time, but we soon found that the inmates started to request replacement boot laces at an alarming rate. No one knew why, until a member of wing staff on night shift decided to sit outside the wing to see what was going on. At about midnight, he saw an inmate hang a shit parcel out of his cell, dangling from a bootlace. He then spun it round and when he had enough momentum, let go. The parcel travelled over the wing roof and landed on the other side, leaving the innocent victims on the opposite section banged up when they should have been associating with each other.

As ever, Rob came up with a solution. As we no longer knew where the parcel had come from, the section bang up would be random. It was a stroke of genius. The stronger boys in each section would threaten the stronger boys in another who would, in turn, put pressure on the rest of the section. The problem soon disappeared.

Another of the roles of the cleaning party was to sort the inmates' dirty clothes and return them to the laundry. The inmates received a change of kit once a week. It consisted of three pairs of underpants, three vests, one pair of jeans, one striped shirt and a set of bedding. All of this was put in a pillow case and hung on the cell door handle. When it was all ready, the cleaning officer would unlock each cell and kick the pillow case into the cell. The inmate would then throw the dirty kit onto the landing for the cleaning party to sort and the cell would be relocked. It doesn't take too much imagination to visualise the state of the underwear after a week in mid-summer, being worn by boys who had no idea about hygiene.

On one occasion, when Colin was the cleaning officer, he took delivery of a box of 100 pairs of new underpants. This was unheard of as most new clothes went to the adult prisons. He took one pair and melted a Mars Bar in the crotch. When the cleaners were sorting out the dirty laundry he asked to see the bag of pants. He pretended to take the Mars Bar pants out of the bag and shouted at them, 'What do you think you are doing? This is too good to waste.' He then promptly ate the melted Mars Bar out of the underpants. One of the cleaning party started vomiting at the sight, prompting the rest of the party to follow suit. I have never seen so much sick in one place.

Colin, without blinking an eye, said, 'Clean this mess up and don't waste perfectly good food again.'

All the cleaners put in a complaint the following morning, but nobody believed their story.

Another memorable incident involved one of the principal officers (whom I shall not name, as it is not the purpose of this book to upset or vilify anybody) who was rather fond of consuming a pint or two at lunchtime. On this particular day, the gate record showed that the PO had returned to the borstal at 2.00 p.m. However, at 4.00 p.m. we started to worry as none of us had seen him. Having contacted control, who sent a radio message out to contact the wing, we received no response. We now started to think that maybe he had been taken hostage. We locked all the inmates up (much to their disgust) and staff arrived on the wing to conduct a search. I was sent to search the laundry room. As we unlocked the door, we were assailed by the smell of dirty underwear. On the bench opposite the door, I could see the pile of soiled underpants rising and falling and making a snoring sound. Using a snooker cue, I cleared the bench of the aforementioned pants to find the PO, flat on his back, fast asleep with a smile on his face, grasping a ham salad roll to his chest and snoring like a hippo. Once he awoke, he ate the roll with gusto without washing his hands and despite it having been covered with badly soiled underwear.

The Old Bailey

As I mentioned earlier, unless you opted out of overtime, you could be called in at any time for extra shifts and this was often as a court escort. On my first rest-day call-in I saw that I was detailed the CCC. I didn't have a clue what this was and asked the Skull. He replied, 'It's the Central Criminal Court, you twit. The Old Bailey!'

The following morning, I reported for duty at 7.00 a.m., unlocked the boy who was going for trial, gave him something to eat and cuffed him up to me. The officer in charge, Dick, then went through the discharge procedure for the inmate and we boarded the taxi and set off for London. All went well at this stage and we arrived at the Old Bailey at about 9.45 a.m. in plenty of time for the court sitting time of 10.30 a.m. We delivered our boy to the cells and went off to find out the duties that we were required to carry out; this could involve supervising any prisoner, in any of the courts. We would collect the lad after the court had risen and take him back to the borstal, if he had not won his appeal.

We were put in a small room in the cell area and given a huge fried breakfast. I then asked Dick what was I supposed to do and he replied, 'When they call Rochester 1, they will be referring to me as I/C, (Officer in Charge) of a dock. You are Rochester 2 and will probably have to do the menial tasks, like running defendants to the various docks.'

Very soon, the tannoy announced, 'Rochester 1 to court

4,' and off he went. I sat there like a pork sausage at a Jewish wedding and when 10.25 a.m. came I thought that I had got away with doing nothing. I then had a wander through the cell area to alleviate the boredom and came across the court principal officer, who looked stressed. I thought it would be friendly to introduce myself, so I did.

He replied, 'Are you Rochester 2?' I replied in the affirmative and he said, 'You stupid fucking bastard. Get yourself up to court 16. You are dock officer I/C and don't ever let me see your fucking face in my court again.'

'Thank you, sir,' I said.

'Don't thank me, you fucking idiot,' he yelled. 'Just get up to the court and do your fucking job.' I immediately detected that he wasn't having a good day, so off I went.

Entering a high court from the cells was bizarre in those days of smoking. You made your way up a set of concrete stairs, trampling on fag packets and butts, to be confronted with an oak door to the court. Once you opened the door into the dock, the magnificence of the British judicial system would overwhelm you: polished oak and people with wigs, but the silence screamed at you.

The judge looked over her specs and said, 'Dock officer, it's very nice of you to attend.'

The defendant was a middle-aged man who had surrendered from bail. I mentally went through my training, took him out of sight, searched him and sat him in the dock facing the judge. He was very upset, but complied. He was a concierge in a large office block who was accused of following a female into the toilets and sexually assaulting her. Unfortunately for him, she turned out to be the wife of a senior police officer. He sat in the dock while the charges were read and was then called into the witness box by the prosecution council. By this time he was in a flood of tears. I guided him to the witness box, which was the size of the average Ford Fiesta, and he completely went to pieces.

The judge said, 'Dock officer, give the defendant a chair.' I looked around and found a portable chair at the back of the court, and she gestured for me to retrieve it. I managed to manoeuvre it, with difficulty, into the witness box and the defendant sat down while I stood behind the box.

With order restored, I waited for the judge to resume the trial, but she continued to look over her glasses at me. After what seemed like half an hour, she appeared to lose her patience and said, 'Dock officer, take a seat.'

I looked around the court and could see no vacant seats. I looked at Her Honour who said, 'It would be nice to continue with these proceedings once you are seated.'

I looked around again, in half-panic and noticed a spare, green, leather judges' chair at the far end of the dais. I stepped up on the dais and sat in the chair, not realising that it was on wheels. It shot off the platform and deposited me on the floor in front of the judge, who by this time had given up the will to live. The only positive that I can take from this is that the previously suicidal defendant had cheered up no end.

When the court rose for lunch I was convinced that I would be sacked before the end of the day, but during the break I received a message that the judge wanted to see me in her chambers. Thinking that I would be charged with contempt of court, I gingerly knocked on her door. Her clerk bade me in and showed me to her sitting room. She looked at me with disdain, turned around to open a cupboard door, shoved a huge glass of single malt in my hand and chatted like a friend for the next hour. It transpired that the court PO, who had threatened me earlier, had explained to her that this was my first time as dock officer and she obviously felt sorry for me. I can't remember much of the rest of the day, as it disappeared in a cloud of scotch.

When the jury retired to consider their verdict, two things would happen in the cells. Firstly, the television was turned on and all staff started to watch *Blockbusters*. Secondly, the senior officer, who was a Savoy-trained chef, started to prepare a meal. I was hoping that the jury would fail to reach a verdict and we could finish watching *Blockbusters* and then have our meal, but a quick, 'open and shut case' verdict came from the court. We considered it an insult to Mr Holness to leave the programme before the end and the smell of the food was just too much. Various excuses were given about the prisoner playing up and when *Blockbusters* had finished we took him to the dock.

The Governors

When I first went to Rochester, the governor was Jack: a really strange man who had no vision for the borstal other than his ambition to man the institution with social workers and get rid of all prison officers. Neither the staff nor the inmates had any respect for him.

In those days, the uniformed officers answered to the chief officer first and the governor second. Unfortunately, the chief officer wasn't really sure what planet he was on and the running of the place was left to those who knew what they were doing. However, despite the management, the discipline was good.

The governor would do his rounds several times a week, but he always tried to avoid B Wing, as whenever he made an instruction, whatever it was, Rob or Bill would say, 'Yes sir,' and then carry on as before. Ultimately, I don't think that he had an issue with this because the team had brought the wing back to a semblance of order, whereas before it had been unmanageable, housing some of the most violent young prisoners in the system.

When an inmate seriously transgressed the rules, he would be placed on governor's report and taken to the segregation unit the following morning. At 10.30 a.m., or when he felt like it, the governor would attend the unit's office to hear the charge that the inmate was accused of, find him guilty or not guilty and (if proven) pronounce punishment. He could award loss of association, loss of earnings or loss of remission (prisoners had to serve two-thirds of their sentence, but could lose time from the other third if they misbehaved).

The amount of time that officers spent sitting in the segregation unit waiting for Jack, who would very often turn up up to two hours late, was ridiculous. He had no respect for his staff or the job that they were trying to do.

On one occasion, a lad was put on governor's report by a member of staff who was on nights. He had caught the inmate passing a small piece of cannabis to the cell next door. He had attached a plastic cup to a length of string and was swinging it out of his cell window. This was at a time when drugs in prisons were rare and governors would be hard on anyone discovered with them. When challenged, the inmate didn't argue, so the officer was satisfied that he didn't need to be there in person at the governor's adjudication.

The following morning, the prisoner was put in front of the governor and pleaded guilty. Jack, at this stage, went into deep thought and said that he could not make a decision without the charging officer being present. So the case was adjourned until the following morning when, after he had finished his night shift, the poor officer had to wait until Jack could be bothered to attend the segregation unit. He finally turned up at about 11.30 p.m., the officer having hung about since his shift finished at 7.30 a.m. Again, the lad pleaded guilty and Jack asked him when the association period finished (one would have thought that he would have known this already). The lad told him that it finished at 8.30 p.m. The governor fell into deep thought once again and in his wisdom, decided that passing a controlled drug was a form of association. The punishment that he went on to

64

award was, 'No association after 9.00 p.m.' It was insane. Luckily, I was standing between the officer and the governor; the officer had such a look of blood in his eyes that he would probably have killed Jack if someone hadn't prevented him.

The governor's complete disregard for staff, the prison system and especially the inmates was demonstrated again when tragedy hit the borstal. I was returning from escort duty and saw a private ambulance driving out of the gate. This usually meant that someone had died and that the body was being removed. Once I relocated my inmate, I was told that two boys had had a fight during a football match and that one had stabbed the other to death. When the orderly officer had gone to the governor's office and informed him, it is reported that he replied, 'I've got someone coming round to repair my washing machine, so I'll have to go home.' And off he went.

Thankfully, the Home Office eventually got wise to the inadequacies of this leader and promoted him to a non-job in London.

When he left, as the social club treasurer, I thought that we should make a collection, even though everyone hated him, so I sent a tin around the borstal for contributions. When it came back to me I was encouraged by the weight. However, when I opened it I found seventeen and a half pence, the contents of a packet of paper clips, several condoms, half a pound of nails and a ferry ticket to France that was three years out of date. We decided to buy him a drink and leave it at that.

When the new governor arrived, the difference was felt by everyone in an instant. Malcolm was a man's man; ex-Blues and Royals, he demanded respect with his demeanour alone. He had worked his way up through the ranks and had a reputation throughout the prison service as being someone that could be trusted. This was underlined by his time in Rochester and he has remained a friend ever since.

An example of the measure of the man can be gained by his reaction when I phoned him to ask if he minded being included in this book. He agreed, but not without confessing that he had a guilty conscience. When I asked why, he told me that when he was governor of Rochester, he was sitting in his office and saw me walking across the parade ground without my cap on. He phoned the orderly officer and told him to drag me in and give me a dressing down. He was later told that I had been in a particularly violent confrontation and was making my way to the hospital wing for treatment. That was over thirty years ago and he still felt guilty!

Malcolm's time in charge was a breath of fresh air. He was upfront, honest and honourable: a trait that is rare in today's self-seeking civil servants. He served as governor until 1987, when the Home Office introduced the 'Fresh Start' scheme (more of this later), deciding that it was a good time to go.

Again, I sent the tin around the borstal as his leaving date approached. But unlike the offering for Jack's departure, he was showered with money, not just from Rochester, but from every institution that he had worked in throughout his career.

On his last day, plans had been made to give him the send-off to end all send-offs. The works officers had built a wooden horse on a four-wheeled trolley and had somehow obtained a sheepskin saddle to put on it. At noon, Malcolm was in his office, signing over the prison to the new governor (Bill – sir to his friends). I waited outside his office and once the official business was done, I escorted him out of the building. Waiting outside was the horse on the trolley with six works officers waiting to pull it, like so many alcoholic steeds. Malcolm was visibly moved as they paraded him on wooden horseback around every part of the prison, eventually arriving at the gate lodge. As the huge double gates were opened, his son (a corporal at horse with the Blues and Royals) was standing in full uniform saluting his father. Behind him, the route from the gate to the social club (some 100 yards) was lined with staff. Rest day or not, everyone turned up, together with scores of people that he had worked with over the previous thirty years. I still see Malcolm about once a year and he always reminisces about this day. He occasionally mentions that they had the sheepskin saddle back to front.

The Gate Lodge and Nights

Everyone who came to or left the borstal had to do so via the gate lodge, which was manned by an experienced officer who recorded all movements in the gate book. The only exceptions to the gate book rule were the members of staff, uniformed or otherwise, who drew keys. Instead, they would give in a tally, inscribed with their key number. The keys were contained in a steel safe, hung on hooks and numbered from number one (the governor) to however many members of staff had been allocated keys. The member of staff coming on duty would hand his tally to the gate officer and would be issued with a set of keys with the corresponding number. Everyone else's movements were entered in the gate book, accompanied by the time in and out.

For some reason, one of the things that I remember from my training is that if an inmate died, he would be entered in the gate book as 'One of the roll, deceased' and when his body left the establishment, he would be entered in the book under 'Contractor's carts'.

Second gate duties were carried out by the most junior staff (i.e. me, an auxiliary officer: a uniformed member of staff who hadn't completed the prison officer training), but were crucial to the running of the institution. The duties consisted of reacting to anyone trying to get in or out of the institution and managing the general flow through the gates, which could be very frustrating because the works office was outside the wall. The officers would come through the gate to march their inmates from parade and then take them through the gate to the works department to collect their tools. They would then bring them back through the gate armed with their tools. Half an hour later, the works officers would come back through the gate to return to the works department for tea break. This would go on throughout the day and each time, the huge gates had to be fully opened, as the party would be pulling trolleys with nothing in them.

One day, I had been detailed second gate, with Bill, as gate officer (not sir to his friends) but a man who had served thirty years as an officer, good at his job and never looking for promotion or praise, and such, because he had no ambition, was a thorn in the side of successive governors, as they couldn't manipulate him. He would often be allocated the gate until he upset someone, which he did at regular intervals. He would then be detailed 8 party, where he couldn't embarrass anyone, until he was forgiven.

Having got over the usual chaos, I put the kettle on, but the peace was disturbed by a rap on the inner gate. It was the chief officer, dressed like Ronnie Corbett in drag, stating that he was going to play golf with the regional director, so we checked him through. However, about five minutes later, Bill said, 'Go and get the chief from the car park. There's an urgent message for him from the Home Office.'

I ran to the car park and the chief was just pulling out, so I walked in front of his car, waving my hands urgently. Once he had stopped, having decided not to run me over, I gave him the message. He was not happy! He parked up, returned to the gate and asked Bill what the panic was. Bill, struggling to keep a straight face, said, 'Rupert bear rang and asked for his trousers back.' I disappeared, but could hear the very unchiefly language from the kitchen.

Bill obviously had a death wish and confirmed it again later that day when the front gate bell rang. On answering it, I saw a huge limo in the road and a guy that looked as though he owned the place. I could see Bill's hackles rise at the sight of him. He looked over his specs at this bloke and said, 'Yes?'

The man in the limo said, 'Lord Stoneham,' and his ID confirmed this.

Bill, with his perverse mind, heard this as 'Lord stone 'em', or so he said and replied 'Is that a hymn or a prayer?'

Back to 8 party for Bill!

When the institution was locked up for the night, the night orderly officer would check that all keys were accounted for, lock the key safe and take the inner gate key so that (although the gate officer could open the outer gate) he had no access to the institution. Depending on who it was, the orderly officer would then deploy the secret weapon (the mattress screwed to a plywood board, as previously mentioned), suspend it between two desks and sleep the night away. But things didn't always go to plan.

On one of my set of nights, with a PO named Ally as orderly officer, we received a message that an inmate, a known psychopath, was getting restless. We went to see him and he told us that he knew when one of his turns was coming on. I gave him a cigarette and then returned to the orderly room to call the duty doctor. He lived about 40 miles away and when I eventually got him on the phone, it was clear that he was having a good time and was more than a little reluctant to attend. We insisted that he attend, as he was being paid a lot of money to be on call, and he eventually agreed.

Several hours later, the inmate had completely lost it. We were rolling round the floor with him, Ally taking a nasty bite on his arm. When the doctor finally arrived at the gate, one of us had to leave the scene to let him in, but this was looking impossible and it took about an hour to calm him enough to be left with one officer. I went to the gate to collect the doctor, who was not only drunk, but furious by this time. I then took him to the segregation wing and introduced him to the inmate, who had started to calm down.

The doctor took one look at him, shouted, 'You ungrateful bastard,' and stabbed his index and middle fingers into his eye sockets. All hell broke loose after that. The doctor and the inmate had become totally uncontrollable. Ally was wrestling with the inmate and I was trying to restrain the drunken doctor. I managed to drag him to the padded cell and I locked the door behind him. When the inmate saw that we were dealing with the doctor, he calmed down and we were finally able to return to the orderly room to complete the paperwork.

When we had gone home after that difficult shift, the senior officer I/C the segregation unit, who obviously had not conducted a proper handover, phoned the orderly officer to say, 'I've got a bloke in the special cell who reckons he's a doctor.' He had just read our report and replied, 'Well, he probably is. Find him someone to cure.'

The chief officer at the time was not the most popular of people. He was mad about crown green bowling and had laid out a bowling green in front of the old gate. It is still there to be seen by anyone who may be interested. He used to spend hours tending it until it resembled a snooker table, but this was an uphill battle because of his unpopularity and the treatment that this attracted. Officers on nights would lead the cows out of the farm and let them trample their way across the green, leaving it looking like the face of the moon. He gave up in the end.

Things would go missing at night, but I'm not suggesting that any of the officers were responsible, as most of them blamed the ghosts of borstal boys long gone. Missing objects would range from plants from the greenhouse to blocks of stone from the car park or sides of bacon from the farm's cold store. However, the piece de resistance was a 2-ton pottery kiln from the education block. The education block was at the back of the institution, as far away from the gate as you could get, surrounded by a 22-foot wall. It was a real enigma and to this day, I haven't got a clue where the kiln went or how it was taken.

Detached Duty

The overall staffing of Her Majesty's Prison Service was overseen by a group of civil servants in Tolworth, Surrey. The guy that dealt with the southeast region was known to all as Worried of Woking (WOW). It was his job to fill holes in one establishment by offering large amounts of expenses to officers from other prisons. This, in turn, would create a shortage in the institution from which the volunteer was taken, thus WOW would ring around and find a member of staff on full expenses to replace the original volunteer. This went round and round, costing the taxpayer more and more, where a temp would have solved the problem. Consequently, there were more prison officers travelling between prisons than there were manning the landings and they would have waved to each other as they passed en route.

My first experience of this was to be sent to HMP Grendon in Gloucestershire for a month. The officer who was there before me was being picked up by his wife. As I didn't have a car, he phoned me and said that if I went on the Saturday, she would give me a lift, but I would have to cover the Sunday late shift. This seemed fine by me. As we drove up to the house, I saw the officer that I was relieving, coming out of the village shop, hand in hand with a very attractive woman. I immediately pointed out the architectural wonders that we were passing, on the other side of the street. Although we nearly crashed into the side of a very beautiful Tudor building, a marriage was saved, albeit for a short time.

Grendon was a strange place, described as a therapeutic institution, catering for prisoners who would normally be in segregation (i.e. sex offenders, informers and those who found it hard to live in a normal prison regime). The Home Office had ordered the opening of a previously mothballed wing, but had supplied no extra staff and it was decided that it would be run on overtime by detached duty staff. I was told that we did not form part of the permanent staff and were not to work anywhere else in the prison other than C Wing.

On my first day, I worked out my shift and at 8.15 p.m., the published time for the end of association, I shouted for the prisoners to bang up and shut the doors behind them. I then walked back to the manor where I was staying, via the local hostelry, feeling quite pleased with myself, as the shift had gone so smoothly. I slept well and reported for duty at 7.30 a.m. the following day.

After serving the prisoners' breakfast, I was told that all staff and inmates attended the wing council meeting at 8.30 a.m. This was something that I had never heard of, but I knew that I could take it in my stride. The meeting was held in the association room and attended by the wing PO, several psychiatrists, a doctor and the vicar. Various wing issues were discussed and when it came to any other business, a prisoner stood up and asked me why I had shut his cell door the previous night. I was gobsmacked and after regaining my composure, explained to the man that the prison service had been charged by the courts to keep him safely in custody; part of this process was making sure that he was securely locked up overnight. The meeting rounded on me, saying that if a prisoner could not be trusted, he would not be at Grendon. I replied that Grendon was a closed prison and if indeed these prisoners could be trusted, they would have been transferred to an open prison. I was then subjected to a patronising lecture from the senior psychologist and felt that it was easier to nod and agree than to tell him what an idiot I thought he was.

At a similar meeting while I was there, a hospital officer was challenged by a prisoner. At the time, no prisoner would challenge a Wandsworth officer without regretting it. The officer's face turned puce and for a while I thought that his head would explode. He stood up and said, 'Listen, you bastards, I carry a bottle in my left pocket for headaches and a bottle in my right one for belly aches; the only choice that you have is to drink from them or wear them!' We never saw him again. I don't think that HMP Grendon was quite prepared for such as he. So he returned to Wandsworth, dispensing from his two bottles.

The wing was run by the principal officer, with total autonomy from the governor who was a psychologist and only interested in how 'The Grendon Experiment' was measured in the main part of the prison. This was certainly different to anything I had experienced before. In fact, I had to accept that I may just have been on another planet. For example, we ran an exercise called the Chief's Party, which was the most pointless exercise that I have ever come across. After the prisoners were unlocked for afternoon labour, they were taken to an open area next to the wing where there was a pile of rubble that was about 12-feet wide and 6-feet high. The party would move this pile, piece by piece, from one end of the yard to the other end. When this was complete, they would be allowed to exercise. The following day, a different officer, who had worked the night shift, would unlock the party, take them to the yard and they would move the pile of rubble to the other end of the yard, where it had been the day before. The odd thing was that this went on for the whole month that I was there and none of us had one complaint from the prisoners.

We worked three twelve-hour shifts and on the fourth day would work a night. On that day we would work from 7.30 a.m. to 5.00 p.m., work a night from 8.30 p.m. to 7.30 a.m. the next day, then return to duty at 12.30 p.m. (to run the Chief's Party) and go off duty at 9.00 p.m., only to start again the next day. At time-and-a-half, it was like writing your own huge pay cheque. I have never seen so much money, but I haven't got a clue what I did with it. There was, however, a problem in those days that we were paid fortnightly, in cash; there was no bank in the village and I had no transport. I arrived home to a pile of bills that had not been paid and no food in the fridge. It is difficult to imagine this situation these days, with BACs credit and debit cards. Perhaps I could have handled it better.

Prison Officer Quarters

All married prison officers were entitled to a prison quarter. This would consist of a one-, two-, three- or four-bedroom house, depending on the size of your family and your rank. Single officers would be housed in the bachelor quarters, known locally as the 'sperm bank'. These would be maintained by the works department and redecorated every three years at no charge to the officer. If a married officer transferred in and there was no available quarter, the head of works would go out and buy one. Although I witnessed this, I often question my memory, as it seems unbelievable in this financial climate. Officers also didn't pay rates or water rates because the quarter became crown land when it was purchased. If an officer had a mortgage, he was paid £25 per week towards his payments and at the end of the year, would receive a rebate on the tax paid on this allowance. This accumulated over three years, until it reached a maximum of £300. So, every year, every officer would receive a payment of £300 in cash. It was great.

What was also great was the fact that officers could retire at fifty-five years old. If they lived in a quarter, they would be issued with an eviction notice by the chief officer and a council house would have already been allocated. They would retire on a half-pay pension, be given a council house and be allowed to draw the dole until they were sixty-five years old, when they would draw a state pension. As a thirty-year-old officer, I was looking forward to my fifties when I could enjoy these benefits. Alas, these disappeared in what Margaret Thatcher described as 'Spanish Practices', but believe me, these could only be British. No other government would countenance these.

At this time I was paying a mortgage on a town house, which was conveniently situated in the city centre. This was easy for my wife to walk to work, as she did not drive. (Later, I did try to teach her, but came near to divorce, either from my lack of teaching skills or her lack of direction/ understanding of the workings of the clutch/control of the car. We had been driving around a large car park in first gear for two weeks and she kept saying that she wasn't ready to drive on the road or change into second gear. She's a lovely lady who has shared my life for the last forty-three years and I would never want to change this unless she asked to take driving lessons again, in which case, I would be honour-bound to report this to the authorities.) The house was also in the perfect spot for my wife to nip down to the shops, it had parkland opposite where the boys could play and, equally as important, it was close to the station. However, the rooms were small and set on four floors and an alleyway that ran past the back of the houses divided the house from quite a large garden. It was difficult for a mother whose husband was at work for ninety hours a week to have eyes in the back of her head, tracking kids who are crawling up and down four floors and not being able to leave the back door open in case they escaped down the alley. Consequently we decided to sell.

We put the house on the market and sold it within two days. This was a bit of a shock, as we had not yet found a suitable property to live in. We set about looking for a home on the Honda N Superdream motorbike that I had bought to get to work, with me steering and my wife clinging on behind. Thankfully, we found the house that we wanted, at the right price and contacted our buyers to tell them that, as soon as we could move to this property, they could complete. Unfortunately, this went on for over a year. The person we were buying from turned out to be a bad debt. Our buyer threatened to drop out and sue us.

The next day at work, I was talking to the clerk of works, who told me that there were more empty quarters than they knew what to do with, due to the freeze in recruiting. We were given the keys to a three-bedroom house where we could live temporarily, which allowed our buyers to complete.

The house was not ideal, as in reality it was only a two-bedroom house with a box room. We stayed there for a few months, living out of boxes, but quite comfortably and rent free. However, after a time, it became clear that, having lived in our own house for so long, this arrangement was becoming fractious. I went to see the clerk of works again, who said, 'Try this one then,' and gave me a set of keys and a site map. At the time, I wondered, if I pushed it, what else he would have up his sleeve.

Soon after, we went to view the property, which was a large, if plain, yellow-bricked, four-bedroom house; three of the bedrooms were large doubles with a reasonably sized single room. We moved in and made an application to the Home Office to buy it. We eventually got it for a ridiculously low price, only to be told by our solicitor that the deeds stated that there was no building on the land (obviously the reason for the low price). It took us a year to sort this out with the land registry.

Control and Restraint

Surprisingly, for staff doing a job with great potential risk, we had minimal training in dealing with violent inmates. The older officers were as hard as nails, with some exceptions, and their responses to attempted assaults usually resulted in the inmate needing treatment in the hospital. Everyone else had to rely on their own sense of self-preservation and the minimal defensive weapons that were provided to get them through. For example, in a riot situation, we were issued with 3-foot staves and were sent in with no other training than having the previously mentioned, rolled-up plimsolls thrown at us.

This was clearly unacceptable, so the Home Office recruited a guy called Tom to train staff, to inflict controlled, minimum pain on violent inmates without inflicting injury. This bloke was an enigma, still remembered by officers who have never met him. He was about 5 foot 10 inches tall and about the same around his belly. He had a broad Norfolk accent and drove a three-wheeled Robin Reliant. On meeting him, he came over as everybody's favourite uncle. What was not obvious was that he was a professor of martial arts and had his own dojo in Japan.

His favourite trick was to get someone to hold a broom, brush side uppermost, with the handle on the ground, 12 inches to his side. He had perfect balance and would kick the broom head clean off without appearing to move. Also, he loved fighting.

Each institution was ordered to send three officers to Lincoln to train in these new techniques. Surprisingly, Rob, who was given the task of choosing, sent me as one of them.

I arrived at a mothballed prison, just outside Lincoln, on a Monday morning to be welcomed by Tom. I found this little old man difficult to take seriously until a well-'ard Wandsworth officer started on him, saying that he didn't come all this way to be shown how to handle prisoners by an old man. We all waited to see what would happen, as I think that we all had similar thoughts but were too polite to say so.

Tom said, 'Come 'ere my booty,' and gave him a 12-inch bayonet then said, 'See what you can do with that.'

The officer tried to keep up his image, but was obviously uncomfortable.

'Come on, lovely boy,' Tom continued. 'You can't do any harm with that.'

The officer then took a half-hearted lunge, largely to keep up his image. Although I was standing about 4 feet away, I didn't actually take in what happened next, but within seconds, well-'ard was lying on his back in an arm-lock with a bayonet at his throat, begging for mercy. Nobody argued with Tom after that. Fortunately, I had learned my lesson at Leyhill and kept quiet.

We saw Tom in action again on the last night of training. We all went for a meal in Lincoln and convened to a local pub for a few drinks. Everyone was happy, but no one was drunk. In the other bar, a bloke had been playing the fruit machine, which hadn't paid out on a win. The guy complained to the barman, who pointed out the phone number on the machine and explained that if the customer made a complaint, he would support him. The customer promptly put a bar stool though a glass shelf.

Hearing the commotion over the bar, Tom said, 'There's no need for that.'

The man shouting back, 'Come round here, Grandad, and get some.' By this time, another four youths were also starting to become aggressive.

By the time I had looked around to see what Tom was going to do, he had disappeared and the idiots in the public bar had gone quiet. A few minutes later, I walked out of the pub to see where Tom had gone and saw the five idiots lying on the pavement, waiting for the police to arrive, crapping themselves.

As the two-week course progressed, we were taught a wide range of techniques and as an ex-rugby player, I was no stranger to a bit of physical contact and took to it like a duck to water. Central to the training was the skill of operating in three-man teams when entering a cell. Number one would hold a shield and would target the weapon. Two and three would enter behind number one and put the prisoner in arm-locks, bringing him forward to the floor. At this point, number one would abandon his shield, once the prisoner had been disarmed, and support the head, removing the prisoner to a place of safety.

We practised this manoeuvre time and time again, and were told that on the last day, each person on the course would take the role of a prisoner in the 'killing room' (his phrase, not mine). We were to be allowed to take any weapon (other than a firearm) in to defend ourselves.

The day finally arrived and we were all led into the 'killing room', which was surrounded by chicken wire so that anything thrown would be contained. I was last in and watched my colleagues, one by one, being taken out, under restraint. When my turn came, I chose a 3-foot piece of scaffold pole and an empty fire extinguisher as weapons. I then waited in the cell for the three-man team to arrive. When they entered the cell I went berserk, crashing into the shield and lashing out with the pole. Eventually, they had to retreat and I felt pretty pleased with myself, completely forgetting the lesson that I thought that I had learned, during basic training, at Leyhill. What I didn't realise was that the exercise was not about my skills, but had been set up by Tom to demonstrate that the most violent prisoner could be controlled by these techniques. He had seen that I would probably get the better of a team under training, so he had his 'A team' standing by.

I thought that I had finished, but as I walked out of the cell Tom said, 'Not so fast, boy. I want to see that again.'

Full of confidence, I stood there with my scaffold pole, ready to teach the next team a lesson, but I didn't even see them enter the cell; they were that fast. The first thing that I was aware of was the shield hitting my right arm and pinning the weapon against the wall. My head was soon between my knees and both my arms in locks. I was then told by the team leader, who was holding my head, that we were going for a walk and was led out of the cell. The one big problem was that he also had his thumb pushed into my windpipe and I was starting to panic to find breath (I found out afterwards that they had been briefed that I was double-jointed and that they were not to believe anything I said, as I would probably break away). I couldn't get any air and was starting to try to free my head. Their reaction was to tighten the lock and I eventually passed out.

When I awoke, I found myself slung over a stable door, my torso inside and my head and shoulders outside, left to fend for myself. The pub was open and the prison service, in those days, was not the place to gain sympathy.

Overall, the techniques that we learned during this training made a huge difference to dealing with violent disorder and some four years later, would be developed further to deal with mass disorder.

When we returned to the borstal, we were told that the regional director had ordered that we put on a demonstration for the governors and members of the board of visitors for the whole of Kent. We set the gymnasium up as an auditorium, using the weights room as a cell, and had planned to take the member of staff from there to the stage. Rob introduced the techniques to the assembled gentry and we proceeded to demonstrate them.

The senior officer who took the role of the prisoner, whom I will refrain from naming, was known for having a well-developed manhood. He paced around the weights room, brandishing a baseball bat and we rushed in to restrain him. He must have gained some satisfaction from this because the more we applied the pain, the bigger his erection became, to the point where it nearly reached his chest. I'm sure that the audience enjoyed it, as the sound of tittering could be heard over his screams. He was known for ever after as Hard On.

Legends in Their Own Lunchtimes

Some of the officers had been working at the borstal since the sixties and a few of them since being demobbed after the war; notably, George and Ernie. They had both served together in the marines and were real characters. I will always be grateful to George, who took me under his wing and taught me more than I ever could have learned from formal training. I never once saw him lose his temper or raise his voice; he demanded respect from both staff and inmates just from his demeanour. He was known by everyone and was one of the first borstal officers to be awarded the Cronin Clasp from the POA (Prison Officers Association). The Cronin Clasp was awarded to people that had given extraordinary and unselfish service to members of the POA.

Ernie, on the other hand, was a nutter.

Twice a week, officers would take the train to London and be driven back with twelve borstal boys from Wormwood Scrubs, so that they could be allocated to suitable borstals. On my first trip, five of us were driven to Rochester Station. As we walked to the platform, Ernie approached the porter and walked away with his cap and broom. He then started sweeping the platform vigorously, making comments to the waiting commuters.

We eventually boarded a train, which was stopping at most stations between Rochester and Charing Cross. There were no seats, so we stood where we could. Ernie stood in front of some poor unfortunate woman reading the paper. He was pretending to grasp a non-existent sling strap all the way to London. At Woolwich Arsenal, a lot of people got off, including the guy who was sitting next to our unfortunate woman. Ernie sat next to her, put his head on her shoulder, smiled at her and said, 'Nice day for a murder.' We bought her a cup of coffee and calmed her down, but by this time Ernie was sweeping the carriages for some reason only known to himself.

Ernie also had his own way of making an impact within the borstal walls. For example, the issue of hair was being reviewed by the governor and Ernie took exception to the outcome. Up to that point, all boys had to have tier haircuts, clear of the ears and neck. The only exceptions were Sikhs, who wore their hair in a top knot and therefore complied anyway. The result of the review was for this practice to cease immediately.

The following day, all the wings marched their boys onto the parade ground as usual, with the chief and the governor presiding. We were all there, standing to attention, apart from A Wing. They were now ten minutes late, which was considered unacceptable. Both the chief and the governor were getting more annoyed, until the sound of perfect marching came from the direction of A Wing. They sounded like the marines, with the shout of 'left, right, left, right' accompanying them. As the A Wing contingent marched perfectly round the corner, Ernie came into sight. He was dressed in a perfectly laundered uniform and marched bolt upright, but flowing from under his cap was a blonde, arse-length wig, flowing in the breeze. As he brought his boys to a perfect halt the whole parade ground collapsed into laughter, except for the governor and the chief. The governor stormed off in disgust and the chief said, 'My office, now!' I don't know what he said to Ernie, but it didn't seem to change him.

When I first arrived at the borstal, reception was run by Bob and Stuart. Any inmate coming in or out of the institution had to go through reception. This is where discharges would be given their civvy clothing, a discharge grant (equivalent to one week's benefit), sign their licence and be issued with information on the firearms act, stating that they could not be in possession of anything capable of launching a projectile for five years. This included a pea shooter. For those coming in, this was the point where their dignity was removed from them. They would submit themselves to a strip search and have all their personal possessions taken from them and stored, other than three books, a radio (as long as it was fitted with an ear piece), a few toiletries and up to a half ounce of tobacco. They may have come in as Jack the Lad, but left looking exactly the same as everyone else.

Bob was a tall, thin, dour man who liked to give the impression that he never smiled. Socially, he had a keen sense of humour, but the boys never saw this side of him. He wore an old-fashioned, uniform greatcoat that went down to his feet and always looked like a supernatural apparition gliding around the borstal. He rarely shouted at the boys, but if he fixed them in a stare it usually did the trick.

Stuart, on the other hand, was a wise-cracking West Ham supporter, who can only be described as a Sergeant Bilko type. He was always setting people up for practical jokes and never slowed down. When the twice weekly batch of newly sentenced borstal boys arrived, Stuart would sit them down in reception and explain what was going to happen to them. His delivery would last about forty minutes and had the effect of putting them at ease, especially those that were frightened, but it was delivered like a stand-up comedy act. It was informative but highly entertaining and comical.

After a while, we started to notice that the officers escorting the boys from their feeder prisons were different every time. We later found out that the speech had become legendary and officers from all over the country were queuing up to man the Rochester escorts so that they could hear it.

Stuart was also adept at making a little extra cash for himself. These were the days of the early video age and he purchased three video players and a stock of tapes to rent out to the rest of the staff. What could possibly go wrong?

One of the younger officers was having a stag night and hired a machine and several soft porn films, of which Stuart had a reasonable selection. He said that he had several deliveries to make and would join them later with the films. As promised, Stuart duly arrived, set up the machine, put on *Debby does Dallas*, poured a beer and settled down to watch it. However, as the fuzzy screen gave way to pictures, the intro to *The Elephant Man* appeared on the screen. Stuart, who by this time had turned a whiter shade of pale, ejected it, raced out of the door, got in his car and roared off. Apparently, he had rented *The Elephant Man* to the chief officer and his wife and must have got the cases swapped.

Overall, the prison service was rife with pranks and misdemeanours and Colin was central to quite a few of them in one way or another. As previously mentioned, he could talk his way out of being hung and I cannot go into every prank that he has pulled on his fellow officers, as this would fill a book on its own. It is not surprising then that he would eventually receive his comeuppance.

Having gone through the selection process, he received a letter from the Home Office promoting him to senior officer at HMP Brixton. His last day at Rochester was an X shift and at 5.00 p.m. we were all waiting in the gate lodge for the roll to be declared correct, so that we could take our meal break. It was a freezing cold February day and what Colin was not aware of was that we had arranged to fill the swimming pool, which would normally be empty until Easter for maintenance.

We all jumped on Colin, lifted him off the ground and then told him that he was going swimming. He was laughing and shouting, 'I'm going swimming,' safe in the knowledge that the pool was empty. When we arrived at the pool, it was dark and he was still blissfully unaware of his impending fate. We grabbed him by his hands and legs and started to swing him.

'One!' He still thought that we were kidding. 'Two!' Still laughing. 'Three!' We let go. When he was 6 feet in the air he turned and saw the water.

'You baaaastaaaards!' he shouted just before he landed in the freezing water. What most upset him was that I had arranged for a medic to be on site, in case he had a heart attack.

Rob also has to be mentioned in this chapter of legends. When I arrived on B Wing as a new screw, I had been in management of some kind for the last thirteen years. I thought that I knew it all and Rob let me make a prat of myself until I realised that I needed help. He then stepped in and built my confidence up. He paired me with Psycho and I truly believe that, had it not been for him, I may well have left. Rob became a good friend and helped me through some difficult times.

Psycho, also known as Ram, also became a good friend. He was Cornish, of which he was proud, but for some odd reason he totally denied that he spoke with an accent. After berating an inmate in pure Cornish, we would take the mickey out of him and he would shout, 'I ain't got an aarccent.'

There are many friends who should be mentioned here, but the best part of thirty-five years and the onset of aging has dulled the memory.

The Social Club

Most of the staff lived in the local quarters, within walking distance of the borstal. Although it would be seen now as almost incestuous, it was a fairly tight and supportive community. The husbands worked up to ninety hours per week and the wives and other family members would support each other.

The centre of the borstal social scene was the social club. Families would gather there on a Friday evening, where there would be a raffle with prizes of meat vouchers, bottles of drink and a roll-over cash prize. There were also many charity events. One that stands out in my memory was a day to raise funds for the local baby unit, inspired by an officer whose child had been born with meningitis and other difficulties. A lot of planning went into this by a lot of people; the Harlequins agreed to play our rugby team, the local jujitsu club booked a world record roof-tile breaking attempt, the local fire brigade agreed to put on a demonstration and we had managed to scrounge free beer from many of the breweries. Many of the officers' wives had agreed to cook food, we acquired marquees from various donors and once it was all set up on the sports field, it looked pretty impressive. Ray, an auxiliary officer, worked his socks off to get everything set up, but unfortunately he started on the discounted beer a little too early.

Several hundred people turned up for the event and

everything was going well. I really can't remember whether the local jujitsu club broke the record, but they frantically ran around, chopping roof tiles with their bare hands and everyone enjoyed it. Then came the rugby match between the borstal team and the Harlequins. The main movers of the team had been boasting that they had been training and would stand a chance, and the first half went well, with the borstal team holding their own. Come half time, the borstal team sat on the grass, trying to get their breath back, while the Harlequins stood around chatting and drinking their orange juice.

The second half was a different story. The stamina of the professionals shone through and they run rings around the home side. However, it was played with a good sense of sportsmanship and when everyone had recovered, the beer started to flow.

The celebrations ran late into the evening and we eventually retired into the club room. A few of us then decided that it would be a good idea to start taking down some of the marquees to save us having to do it the following evening. When we had taken down the first one and tightly rolled it up, we found that it would not fit into its case. We then noticed that the lump of canvas was snoring. On unrolling it, we found none other than Ray, sound asleep and blissfully unaware of what was going on. We tucked him up under another piece of canvas and let sleeping auxiliaries lie.

Several times during the year, the social club committee would book concert nights. Normally they would be stars of the sixties: The Love Affair, Danny Williams (of 'Moon River' fame), Mike Berry and many others that I cannot recall. These were good, fairly inexpensive nights out that were enjoyed by all who attended, underlining the club's function as a community centre. However, the club really came into its own during the run up to Christmas and it all started on bonfire night.

The construction of the bonfire would begin in September in the field opposite the club. By the time 5 November came along, it would be about 15 feet high and the same across. The committee also purchased over £1,000 worth of fireworks and had members trained in pyrotechnics.

On the night itself, there would be several hundred people gathered around the barriers set up to stop people wandering near the fire. These consisted of staff members and their extended families and any locals who wished to attend. At 7.30 p.m. the pile was dowsed with petrol and lit, followed by the firework display, which was always impressive and lasted about an hour. The families would then repair to the bar where hot food was laid on and, inevitably, the beer would flow.

From September, the committee would start selling raffle tickets for the Christmas grand draw. All the income was spent on prizes and by the time of the draw, the week before Christmas, they would amass thousands of pounds worth of goods, including the latest televisions, video players and other appliances, together with several hundred bottles of spirits.

The weekend before the draw was the children's party. The club would buy a present valued at around £5 (not to be sneezed at thirty-odd years ago) for each member's child under the age of ten, which would be given at the party. The afternoon would start with all the youngsters sitting on the floor, facing the stage, being whipped up into a frenzy by one of Santa's elves, who was over 6 feet tall and built like a brick outhouse. But, dressed in green with a bell on his hat, it seemed to fool the kids.

The little ones were told that Santa was still in Lapland and would only come if he could hear them shouting his name, so the noise grew louder and louder, with shouts of 'Santa, Santa', while Santa (Lee) was getting changed in the kitchen.

Lee took this responsibility very seriously and would have been mortified if he destroyed the Christmas dreams of any of the children. But, every year, he would work himself up into a confusion of self-doubt and every year he would apply the same remedy: he would pour half a bottle of whisky down his neck and instantly transform into the real Father Christmas. Once he was sufficiently lubricated, he would enter the club room with the sack of gifts over his shoulder, accompanied by his elves (who would have shamed the Krays into changing their bodyguards).

Lee would always do his homework, finding out if anything had changed in the child's life since last year and telling them that he had noticed it on his last visit. My four-year-old son had moved bedrooms that year and Santa told him that if it happened again, he should write and tell him to prevent his presents going to his brother. He was so convincing that all the kids used to boast that they had seen the real Father Christmas.

After all the gifts were given out, Santa would disappear through the back door to cheers from the children and from, by this time, the well-lubricated off-duty officers. Five minutes later, Lee would appear with a pint in his hand. One year, he still had a pure white eyebrow over one eye.

Each year, the committee would book a professional

98

pantomime troupe to entertain the older children. After Santa had done his bit, everyone would move to the function room where the players had set up and were ready to start the show. The children sat in the front and the adults stood behind. These shows were always excellent and the children always joined in the fun, but not as much as the fathers, who by this time had got the taste. Cries of 'He's behind you', 'Oh no he didn't' and 'Oh yes he did', rang out into the early hours, long after the troupe and the children had gone home.

The celebrations culminated with New Year's Eve. This was an adults-only night. The older children on the estate could name their price as babysitters and did. The celebration usually consisted of a disco and after the New Year had been seen in, the party usually continued at one of the quarters.

One year, an officer who had overdone it turned up for duty in the segregation wing the following morning, having come from a party an hour before. We put him in the special cell to sleep it off and forgot about him. That night, the night staff, thinking that they were dealing with a violent inmate kicking the door, were surprised to see a slightly dishevelled officer walking out of the cell.

The End Game

In the 1982 Criminal Justice Act, the Government announced that the borstal system would end after seventy-four years and be replaced with the young offender system. The borstals, though not perfect, had transformed many boys' lives. Lads would come to us, never knowing any structure in their lives and never having experienced discipline of any sort, and the experience would change them. I remember several examples of boys having to be physically removed from the institution on the day of their release, as they did not want to return to the chaos that was their lives. Some were completely illiterate when they were sentenced and left able to read and write, and had learned a trade.

The above paints a rosy picture of borstal life, but this represents those boys that wanted to accept help. Conversely, many of the boys would see their sentences through and then carry on as before after their release. In fact, the first borstal boy that I spoke to in A Wing, Rochester, was also the last prisoner that I saw when I retired from Maidstone Prison in 2005. He had spent all his adult life committing petty crime to fund a drug and alcohol habit.

I believe that there were two main reasons for ending the borstal system. The first, understandably, was that personal officers would determine the length of sentences and not the courts. The second and most important was that it was expensive. The cost of providing fully equipped, vocational training workshops and paying salaries to the instructors, and providing a full-time education unit, fully staffed with qualified teachers, would have been huge. This was the beginning of the age of political spin.

The borstals were to be rebranded young offenders institutions (YOIs). In fact, various 'new-speak' policies were bandied about by the Home Office, who invented phrases like 'meaningful activities for all YOIs'. What this translated as, in my experience, was lads packing up Mr Men books in polythene for six hours a day instead of learning a trade.

The clever people at Whitehall also invented 'Prindus' (prison industries). There were several industrial prisons, like HMP Coldingley, that had successful workshops, producing such things as road signs. They had been successful for years and the powers that be decided that this would be disseminated to the rest of the estate. Someone up top then decided that they would start producing different products that seem to be easily categorised as anything that could be thrown at staff during a mass disturbance. This included Bakelite ashtrays and toothbrushes with low-density, plastic handles, allowing the little darlings to melt them and insert razor blades, transforming them into a very effective weapon. There were other idiotic products that escape my memory and 'Prindus', thankfully, faded into memory fairly quickly.

After the end of the borstal system, in 1983, I served at Rochester YOI, until August 1988. Ram and I transferred to the newly built HMP Swaleside, on the Isle of Sheppy, to taste the poison cup of the adult system. I then moved to HMP Maidstone in 1994, retiring in 2005. I look on my time in Rochester Borstal as the happiest time in my years of service, enriched by the characters that I worked with, the antics of some detailed in this book. However, I try not to look at this period through rose-coloured specs and although these characters were unique, I try to evaluate my life and recognise that when one character disappears, another one comes on to the scene. I have been fortunate to work with some interesting people, both staff and prisoners (some of whom have been the subject of successful films and books), and have made some lifelong friends.

I am often asked how I worked with some of the most violent people in society.

I would say to anyone asking this question, 'Don't judge anyone, until you know them and even then, prepare to admit that you are wrong.'